The Fires of '88

YELLOWSTONE PARK & MONTANA IN FLAMES

OVIS—J. VANUGA

by Ross W. Simpson

AMERICAN GEOGRAPHIC PUBLISHING
MONTANA MAGAZINE

Acknowledgments

My very special thanks to Carolyn Zieg Cunningham, editor of *Montana Magazine,* for whom I have written articles the past couple of years. Cunningham convinced Rick Graetz at American Geographic Publishing that I was the one to write this book. Accept my heartfelt thanks, Carolyn, for believing in me.

To Bill Brock, a reporter for the Bozeman *Daily Chronicle,* who spent two days digging through the morgue file at his newspaper, copying every article ever written on the fires at Yellowstone National Park. The information gleaned from those stirring accounts helped me fill in many blank spaces, especially dates that tend to become blurry after inhaling enough carbon monoxide to make one "brain dead."

To Frank Mosbacher, the chief information officer for the Greater Yellowstone Unified Fire Command, who always had the latest information about winds, rate of fire spread, and anecdotes on the tip of his tongue no matter what time of day or night.

To Jim Brass, Project Manager for NASA's High Altitude Aircraft Program, for providing some stunning aerial photography from LANDSAT and ER-2, an enhanced version of the U-2 spy plane that flew six missions over the park during the fires.

To Andy Beck, the architect who supervised the restoration of Old Faithful Inn, for providing photographs of the B-17 and B-47 that crashed in Yellowstone.

To George Robinson, Chief Naturalist at Yellowstone National Park, and district naturalist Joe Halliday for putting the devastating fires into their proper perspective. Sometimes, fellas, it's difficult to see the forest for the burning trees.

To Emily Anderson and Amy Vanderbilt in the Public Information Office at Yellowstone National Park Headquarters in Wyoming, thanks for providing me with a paper trail on the "Long Hot Summer," including maps and post-fire reports.

To Donna St. John at the Veterans Administration in Washington who turned up the name of a World War II airman who survived a plane crash in Yellowstone National Park.

Thanks, too, to Sonny Ueberroth, my editor at Mutual Broadcasting System, who dumped every byte of information about the fires into my computer while I was away from the office, and Bart Tessler, Vice President of News at Mutual, for sending me on such exciting assignments.

I flew to Yellowstone to cover the fires after spending five hair-raising days and nights investigating street-gang violence in Chicago, and from the fires in Yellowstone, I hurried to Texas and Mexico in time to greet Hurricane Gilbert as he came ashore near the seaside town of San Fernando, 120 miles south of Matamoros.

And finally, to my lovely wife, Judy, who kept the "home fires burning" while I drank my fill of excitement that September, thanks from the bottom of my heart.

RWS

ISBN 0-938314-66-1

© 1989 American Geographic Publishing, Box 5630, Helena, MT 59604. (406) 443-2842

Text © 1989 Ross W. Simpson

Design by Len Visual Design; Linda Collins, graphic artist

Printed in U.S.A.

About the author

Ross W. Simpson is an award-winning network radio correspondent with the Mutual Broadcasting System in Washington, D.C.

He has served as congressional correspondent at

ROSS SIMPSON PHOTO

Mutual, covering both the House and Senate, and as floor reporter at the Democratic and Republican national conventions.

Currently, Simpson anchors the evening news on the Mutual Radio Network and is heard from coast to coast and overseas on the Armed Forces Radio Network.

In addition to his anchor duties, Simpson logs more than 30,000 miles per year covering major news stories—such as the 1988 fires in Yellowstone National Park.

He is married to the former Judith Holdren and has four children, two of whom are in college.

The author and his family live in Haymarket, Virginia.

Contents

OVIS—J. VANUGA

MICHAEL H. FRANCIS

STEVE DOWELL; BOZEMAN DAILY CHRONICLE

Clockwise from top: Sunset at Pelican Creek caps another day of firefighting in Yellowstone, 1988. Smoke on the horizon is from the Snake River Complex.

Hours after fires raged through this stand of lodgepole pine near Madison, a young elk browses in the ash.

Sometimes all that firefighter could do was stand and watch Mother Nature vent her fury on the forest.

Author Ross Simpson taking a breather at Old Faithful Geyser.

Title page: The Red-Shoshone fire seen from Yellowstone Lake near Lake Lodge.

Front cover, background: The North Fork Fire crowns near Willow Park. (MICHAEL & BARBARA PFLAUM) ***Inset, left:*** Helicopter with water bag at Swan Flat. (OVIS—J. VANUGA) ***Inset, right:*** A weary firefighter (WILLIAM R. SALLAZ)

Back cover, top: Burned timber is the background for an elk's "bugling" mating call. (OVIS—J. VANUGA) ***Bottom:*** Firefighters evacuate a mountain camp as the Storm Creek Fire advances. (MICHAEL CRUMMETT)

Foreword

Two firefighters silhouetted against a forest fire as darkness fell in Yellowstone.

One of a hundred crew bosses who supervised personnel in hand-to-hand combat against the fires.

The heat, drought and fires of 1988 became very real to me during the Canyon Creek Fire in Montana's southern Scapegoat Wilderness. I was scheduled to guide a backpacking trip into the Danaher Basin country of the Bob Marshall Wilderness the last week in July. "The Bob" is contiguous to the Scapegoat.

A couple of weeks before the trip, smoke started rising over the Continental Divide to the west of Helena from the drainage of the North Fork of the Blackfoot River, the trailhead I was to use into the Bob Marshall. Early observations reported the fire was moving slowly northeast into the wilderness and the trail should be fine for the trip. I checked again several days before leaving and found that high winds had pushed the fire in all directions and the trailhead was closed. We went into the Danaher via another route.

From the Danaher Meadows we watched smoke from Canyon Creek grow into a voluminous column forming a cumulus cloud. When the upper winds caught the top, it developed an anvil head.

Normally in late July the Danaher is in full bloom displaying lush green grass and wildflowers and offering excellent fishing. This year the grass was tinder-dry, brown, and it crackled under our feet. The water was too warm to support good fishing and hiking during the middle of the day was a major effort. We knew then the summer of '88 was not going to be normal.

I was also hearing of the fires in Yellowstone Park and became dismayed because much of Yellowstone is favorite hiking and ski touring country for me. In August we made a backpacking trip into Montana's Madison Range and experienced the same dry conditions as in "the Bob," but no fires. Fortunately, with the winds prevailing from the west, the Madison Range was clear of smoke. From the summits we could see the towers of smoke coming out of Yellowstone to the southeast.

As August went on, the fires in Yellowstone grew worse and a trip into the Jackson Hole country and the Wind River Range of Wyoming was marred by smoky skies, mostly from the Yellowstone blazes.

I didn't venture into Yellowstone in summer 1988...news reports gave the impression that the whole park was lost. As the fires began to subside in late September, I made my first trip to Yellowstone to see what had happened.

With the help of the Park Service I was able to cover much of the country on the ground and by helicopter. Surprise! The entire park hadn't burned as the national news had indicated. And, in fact, I found exciting and interesting changes. Vistas that had heretofore been blocked by dense stands of lodgepole pine were now open...new meadows were being created. From the air I could see mosaics of green and black and noted that not even half of the park had been touched. I was also happy to see that out of the part that had burned, a large share was subject only to groundfire that would quickly come back in grass.

Certainly there were some first-degree burns to be seen, especially in the Madison River country and to the east of West Yellowstone, but here again views were opened up and the following summer a profusion of wildflowers and grasses would take the place of blackened ground. Once the burned snags of the forests are bleached out, they blend in with a beautiful landscape of green grass and new trees coming to life.

In Yellowstone, I also had an opportunity to visit with many people, including businessmen and park officials. Everyone had opinions. My friend Len Sargent, a rancher from Corwin Springs, Montana, a small community just to the north of Yellowstone's northern entrance, had some of the wisest comments. He said, "the fires had their own you-can't-stop-us policy." He also allowed that "lost income and smoke can transform ordinary citizens into Ph.D. biologists with 30 years of experience based on nothing." He also said that "angry people don't think and it is human nature to jump on someone when something goes wrong." In this case it was William Penn Mott, Director of the Park Service, and Bob Barbee, Superintendent of Yellowstone National Park. Len was right, and I guess you can't blame people who see their businesses hurting and favored vistas going up in smoke for reacting negatively. One hopes, though, that much of the anger is subsiding and people can see what good will come to the area.

Now is the time to take advantage of what we have, a new Yellowstone reborn in some areas and unchanged in others. The wildlife, thermal features, fabulous Grand Canyon of the Yellowstone and spectacular scenery are still there and a new dimension has been added. Visitors for years to come will observe the park gradually changing. This will be an opportunity for photographers to record the new Yellowstone and then follow it each year as the vegetation regenerates.

This book details the events of the dramatic Fires of '88. Enjoy it, learn from

USDA FOREST SERVICE

STEVE DOWELL; BOZEMAN DAILY CHRONICLE

it and explore what has taken place. And, if you have children, make sure they see the results of this historic event...it is something they will remember for the rest of their years.

Rick Graetz
Helena, Montana

Above: New growth springs up days after the fires, even with stubborn fire eating away at a tree trunk. *Top:* Healing snow cover was welcome in autumn 1988.

A hot time at Old Faithful

PATRICK CONE

The first time I saw the 1988 Yellowstone fires was on August 26, while flying from Billings, Montana to Salt Lake City, Utah with Republican vice presidential nominee Dan Quayle.

From the left side of Quayle's campaign plane, I saw columns of dirty brown smoke boiling up to our cruising altitude of 30,000 feet.

The 727 charter aircraft flew along the edge of the fire for 15 minutes. That's how big the fire was. Little did I know that in less than two weeks I would be on the ground staring a ferocious firestorm in the face at Old Faithful.

"Yeah, it was scary. A frightening place to be," said firefighter Dave Ullrich as he watched a 200-foot-high wall of flame roll over the newly resurfaced road to Craig Pass and slam into the southern end of the Old Faithful complex on September 7.

The flames had forced Ullrich and his men to abandon their positions in the timber above the Montana Power substation at Old Faithful.

"At first we thought it [the fire] would spot around *us,* and we'd be able to pick it up," said Ullrich as he recounted his close call, "but then a wall of flame hit our position. There was no choice but evacuate as fast as possible."

Gale-force winds—clocked at 50 miles per hour, gusting to 65 miles per hour—sent a firestorm raging across Old Faithful.

Animals became confused in the smoke. An elk cow and her calf ran onto a highway, a glazed look in their eyes, not knowing which way to run. A herd of bison thundered into a meadow to escape the flames that had turned from brilliant orange to ugly purple.

Dave Ullrich was right. It's scary to find yourself staring at a wall of flames. I was the only reporter in the timber when the ridgeline went up in flames, and here are some of the on-scene reports I recorded as the fire roared through the timber:

"There's a war going on here in Yellowstone National Park near Old Faithful. Three helicopters are dumping slings of water on the ridge above me. The smoke is beginning to boil up to fifteen, twenty thousand feet. It's reddish brown. Blotting out the sun..."

"You can sense the fire is getting very close. It's getting dark. Almost like night, but it's the middle of the afternoon..."

"The fire is now licking over the top of the ridge. You can feel the wind. This is

The firestorm was kicking up so much ash and smoke, it was almost impossible to see the helicopters as they tried to halt the fire headed toward Old Faithful.

Clouds of smoke billowing over the mountains surrounding Old Faithful.

Facing page: *The benches at Old Faithful Geyser were empty as a firestorm swept over the southern end of the Old Faithful complex on September 7, 1988.*

what drives that fire like a racehorse across these ridges and through these canyons."

I was with a fire team from Alabama. A team from Texas was on the right flank. Behind us in the maintenance yard were several engine crews hosing down the fuel dump and wooden structures with foam. The area looked like a war zone.

Overhead in the dense smoke we could hear the "whump, whump, whump" of Huey and Chinook helicopters carrying canvas buckets full of water from the nearby Firehole River.

The firestorm was kicking up so much ash and smoke, it was almost impossible to see the helicopters as they tried to halt the fire headed toward Old Faithful. Looking up through the smoke you could barely see the sun hanging in the sky like a fireball filtered by the smoke. The scene reminded me of an eclipse.

Weather forecasters had predicted strong winds for Wednesday, but Denny Bungarz, the incident commander on the North Fork Fire (which included Old Faithful), confessed the wind's velocity was beyond anyone's expectations.

In addition to high wind, there also was low humidity. "Seven percent," said Bungarz, "and those of you in the firefighting business know that's very low."

When the fire roared out of Black Sand Basin and made a bee-line for Old Faithful, it preheated fuels ahead of it, causing us to feel the wind at our backs. The wind was cyclonic. Many trees snapped like toothpicks, some 15 to 20 feet off the ground. They looked like

someone had detonated explosive charges on their trunks. One of the pine trees that fell before the flames was 18 inches in diameter.

Being in a firestorm is like being in a hurricane. The only difference: FIRE instead of RAIN blows in your face. As the wind increased in velocity, the light around us changed rapidly from orange to sepia to gray. It got dark at three o'clock in the afternoon when the wind shifted and drove flames from a ridge west of Old Faithful into a drainage that runs south of the complex. A sinister darkness settled over the timber.

For a young man and woman on the Alabama fire team, this was their "baptism by fire." Elizabeth Parks and Ricky Kerr, both from Talledaga, never had seen fire like this back home. "But it wasn't scary," said Parks as she laughed nervously. "It was only scary if you were scared of IT," added Kerr.

When the firestorm rolled over their position on September 7, and drove them back to the maintenance yard where other firefighters were hosing down the fuel dump and wooden buildings with foam, the team from Alabama had been "on the line" at Yellowstone for 22 days.

Crew chief Art Goddard, from Montgomery, had fought forest fires before, but nothing like this. "These are historic weather conditions we're confronting," said Goddard as he ordered Parks and Kerr to begin digging a hand line near the substation. "I'll probably never see another fire like this in my lifetime."

The most critical part of fighting for-

7

est fires is communication. "Keeping ourselves aware of where we are and where the fire is," said Goddard as he counted heads of those team members who had retreated from the timber. "We always try to keep the fire in our face, never let it outflank us and get behind us."

Alabama team leader Charles Lee, from Andalusia, knew his people were fighting a losing battle with Mother Nature. "We've got so much heavy fuel on the ground, low humidity and high winds," shouted Lee as he ordered his people to head for waiting trucks and hightail it out of the maintenance yard, "that we couldn't hold the fire back."

Just before the fire teams from Alabama and Texas fell back to the maintenance yard, the district supervisor called in an air strike.

Smoke from Yellowstone's Mink Creek Fire was heavy in the southern Absaroka Mountains north of the park.

I watched the aerial tanker make its approach and filed the following report for the Mutual Broadcasting System, one of 200 on-the-scene reports I filed during the next eight days at Yellowstone:

"A Forest Service lead plane coming in through the smoke; dipping its wings, setting up the angle of attack for a DC-6 tanker plane. We're looking right down its props. He's coming right into our face. Here it comes. In low. About 250 feet above the trees. Drop set. [Sound of four-motor propeller-driven plane passing directly overhead.] And away goes the retardant! A cloud of magenta chemicals falling into the burning timber, the second and last salvo this bomber has made."

Tanker planes can carry up to 3,000 gallons of the pink retardant in a cargo

bay beneath their bellies. There are eight "gates" or trap doors in that compartment. The person calling in the air strike can order a two-, four-, six- or eight-gate drop.

If the fire is burning intensely in a small area, the plane can drop the entire load. In this particular case, the fire was burning intensely, but it was spread out along the entire ridgeline, so the bomber made two passes, dumping half its load on each pass.

The retardant had little or no effect on the fire. As soon as the sticky pink chemical hit the ground, the fire flinched for a few seconds, went WHOOSH! and roared back to life again. It was obvious to everyone present that Mother Nature was going to have her way. The fire was like a runaway freight train at Old Faithful. UNCONTROLLABLE!

By the time Charles Lee and the rest of the Alabamans withdrew under fire, burning embers from the raging inferno were falling in the maintenance yard. Some of the embers were the size of a man's hand.

It took fewer than 30 minutes for the firestorm to sweep across the ridge above the power substation and penetrate the perimeter of the Old Faithful complex. That's how fast the firestorm moved.

When forecasters predicted high winds for Wednesday, September 7, orders were issued to evacuate the Old Faithful complex for the first time in its 116-year history.

Wendy Morrison of Scottsdale, Arizona said a bellman knocked on her door at 6:45 A.M. and told her the National Park Service was evacuating the area. Morrison and other guests at the Old Faithful Inn were told to leave the area by 10 A.M.

In all about 500 to 600 people were asked to leave. Non-essential employees—those who worked in the other two lodges, a general store and service station—had until noon to get out. But there was no panic.

In fact, tourists driving down from West Yellowstone, 30 miles away, were allowed to enter the complex in mid-afternoon, hours after the evacuation was ordered, and only 10 minutes before the firestorm struck. Why endanger so many lives?

District Ranger Joe Evans said, "We were offering tourists the opportunity to get from West Yellowstone to Jackson [Wyoming] over Craig Pass."

At the time, Evans felt the park was safe, but after the firestorms he admitted, "I think we got a little closer to the edge than we're normally comfortable with."

When a fire like the one that roared

Smoke provides a backdrop for high school football practice at West Yellowstone, Montana.

into Old Faithful is burning at full steam, experts say it is releasing the energy equivalent of 3 trillion BTUs per square mile, enough energy to heat 4,300 homes for a year. But close to the fire, it's cold as the cyclonic winds suck the air away from you and the day turns to night. I can remember shivering and shaking.

The high winds forced the smoke to the ground around the Old Faithful complex. Those of us who stayed behind to report on the firestorm ran into the Old Faithful Inn, grabbed linen napkins from dining tables and made masks of them.

The smoke not only made it extremely difficult to breathe, but also burned your eyes. Somehow, tobacco smoking didn't seem so harmful after inhaling this much smoke and ash.

At times the wind was blowing so hard, you had to hang onto your hard hat.

If there are ever any medals handed out for service "above and beyond the call of duty" at Old Faithful, three farmers from Ashton, Idaho certainly deserve some. They installed an irrigation system that saved the Montana Power substation that provides electricity to keep the Old Faithful complex, the park's number-one tourist attraction, in business.

One of the three, Dale Clark, said he got a call from the National Park Service at 10 P.M. Monday, September 5, two days before the firestorm struck at Old Faithful. "By two P.M. Tuesday," said Clark, "we had the main line in and the laterals in operation."

Clark and his friends also installed a water cannon that hosed down the de-

energized substation. As the fire roared along the ridgeline above the facility, Clark said, "All we can do now is make sure the pumps don't quit." They didn't, and the $5 million facility was spared.

If the 50,000-volt substation had been knocked out, repair crews, who replaced only a couple of power poles, some insulators and about 55 feet of power line, said it would have taken at least a year to replace the transformers.

Had the substation been lost, Old Faithful would not have re-opened for the winter tourist season on December 14, and concessionaires, those who operate the lodges, would not have recouped some of the tourist dollars lost when they were forced to shut down a month early in September.

"We really lucked out," said Harold Bouse, a division foreman for Montana Power Company, as he supervised the installation of power poles and line.

Dale Clark was joined by more than 100 Mormon farmers and college students from Idaho who dropped what they were doing at home, and laid miles of irrigation pipe to provide a wet buffer zone between the town of West Yellowstone, Montana and the North Fork Fire.

Despite economic losses they suffered while away from home at harvest time, Clark said the sacrifice was worth it. "It's never a hardship to help out," he said.

Thanks to heroic acts by more than 200 firefighters, civilian and military, who manned 17 engines and made up four 20-man fire teams, Old Faithful was spared

SCOTT CRANDELL

Road obviously closed to the community of Duck Creek north of West Yellowstone. One look at smoke on the horizon is enough warning.

Modern fire management in Yellowstone National Park dates back to 1963 when the Leopold Report was released. That report urged that natural areas of the National Park System be administered as "Vignettes of Primitive America." In other words, natural fires were encouraged.

In 1972, Yellowstone was one of several national parks to initiate its own program to allow natural fires to run their course. The plan was being refined in the spring of 1988 when fires began to erupt.

Yellowstone's fire management plan has four goals:

1. To permit as many lightning-caused fires as possible to burn under natural conditions.

2. To prevent wildfire from destroying human life, property, historical and cultural sites, special natural features or threatened and endangered species.

3. To suppress all man-caused fires (and any natural fires whose suppression is deemed necessary) in safe, cost-effective and environmentally sensitive ways as much as possible.

4. To resort to prescribed burning when and where necessary and practical, to reduce hazardous fuels, primarily dead and downed trees.

From the time the plan went into effect in 1972, until the fires broke out in 1988, a total of 34,175 acres burned in the park due to natural fires. The largest fire consumed about 7,400 acres.

It is not uncommon in the spring and summer for thousands of lightning bolts to strike Yellowstone, but most strikes simply fizzle out with no acreage burned.

Mother Nature broke all of the rules in 1988.

heavy damage. Park officials calculated firefighting efforts saved some $70 million it would have cost to replace structures at the complex.

As darkness fell over the compound on September 7, Incident Commander Denny Bungarz and District Ranger Joe Evans held an outdoor news conference to tally up the cost. "The fire that swept across the southern end of the complex destroyed 14 rustic cabins, six of which were not in use and condemned," said Bungarz.

Amy Beesel lost virtually everything she owned. Her cabin was one of those destroyed in the firestorm at Old Faithful. Ironically, the Pittsburgh native working for the park concessionaire had moved into the cabin just three days before.

Beesel had been told by her bosses at TW Services that she and other non-essential employees had until Thursday, September 8, to leave the area. Thinking she had plenty of time, Beesel rode to the Jackson airport with friends.

When they returned, they found Old Faithful under fire and the roads closed. A friend on a motorcycle was able to retrieve a bag of clothing, but all of her expensive photographic gear and irreplaceable photos and negatives were destroyed.

A storage building also was lost, including the gasoline tanker truck and two abandoned autos inside the shed.

The fire was so intense it melted the rubber off the wheels of the truck and cars, shattered the windshields and scorched off the paint. Only their rusty-looking hulks rested among a heap of smoldering ashes.

In the government area of the Old Faithful complex, two small rustic cabins burned to the ground. The old dormitory building suffered damage to the second floor. That was the negative side of the firestorm.

"On the positive side," said Bungarz, "nobody was hurt." And the danger at Old Faithful was over. "The area has been fire-proofed for years to come," said the incident commander, "but the bad thing is it burned a lot of trees around the area." More than 56,000 acres went up in flames on September 7.

At one point on that date, the Old Faithful complex was completely encircled by a ring of fire. Every ridgeline around the famous geyser was burning. The complex was cleared of all non-essential people after dark, and everyone, including the media, was escorted north to Madison Campground and West Yellowstone.

The convoy drove down the center

lane of the highway through a gauntlet of fire for more than 10 miles. The hillsides on both sides of the road were blazing. It wasn't until we returned the following day that we could see the extent of damage.

There were a lot of unhappy people at Old Faithful the day after the firestorm. Don Edgarton, who manages the photo shops, was furious. He claims only cosmetic work was done at Old Faithful. "They're [fire crews] going around the campgrounds saving restrooms and old cabins. We've got 10 million trees that are gone. They ain't saving none of them."

Edgarton was aggravated that the hand crews didn't attack spot fires just east of the observation point. "They let the photographic backdrop to the world's most famous geyser burn," said Edgarton as he shook his head in disgust. "We're sick about what's happened to the forest, because we don't believe it's going to come back in three, four or five years."

Personnel including Incident Commander Bungarz of the U.S. Forest Service deny they "fiddled" while the park burned. "We have fought this fire aggressively from day one [when it broke out in the Targhee National Forest in Idaho] and the Park Service has let us put in tractor lines and sprinkler systems where we needed them," said Bungarz.

"Would a battalion of army regulars have been able to stop that spot fire [east of the geyser]—would a tractor stop it?" asked Bungarz, who answered his own question. "Only a mile-wide fire line could have stopped the firestorm from spotting at Old Faithful and burning the ridgeline beyond the observation point."

"There's a lot of folks who can second-guess, that's easy to do," said Bungarz as he fielded questions from reporters outside his command post at Old Faithful, "but I just feel as the Incident Commander, I've been given all of the latitude I need to fight this fire."

"If I had been able to second-guess," laughed District Ranger Evans, who stood beside Bungarz in the glare of television lights, "I wouldn't have lost $2,000 in the stock market." Both Bungarz and Evans said they didn't think heads should roll in the wake of the Yellowstone fires, but believed that policy and its implementation needed to be looked at.

"I don't think blame can be laid on one man," said Evans. "I don't think that's fair. Bob Barbee [Superintendent at Yellowstone National Park] is in a tough job."

"Do you think there's something wrong with the policy?" shouted a reporter. While Evans refused to answer the question yes or no, he did say decisions were made based upon 100 years of fire behavior and weather conditions in Yellowstone. And that's where an investigating team concluded National Park Service personnel erred.

For example, a team of National Park Service and U.S. Forest Service fire experts concluded that the Storm Creek Fire

Historic Old Faithful Inn was spared as a firestorm cut across the southern side of the complex.

11

PRELIMINARY SURVEY OF BURNED AREAS:
YELLOWSTONE NATIONAL PARK AND ADJOINING NATIONAL FORESTS
GREATER YELLOWSTONE POST-FIRE RESOURCE ASSESSMENT COMMITTEE, BURNED AREA SURVEY TEAM

OCTOBER, 1988
(Burned areas as of Sept. 15, 1988)

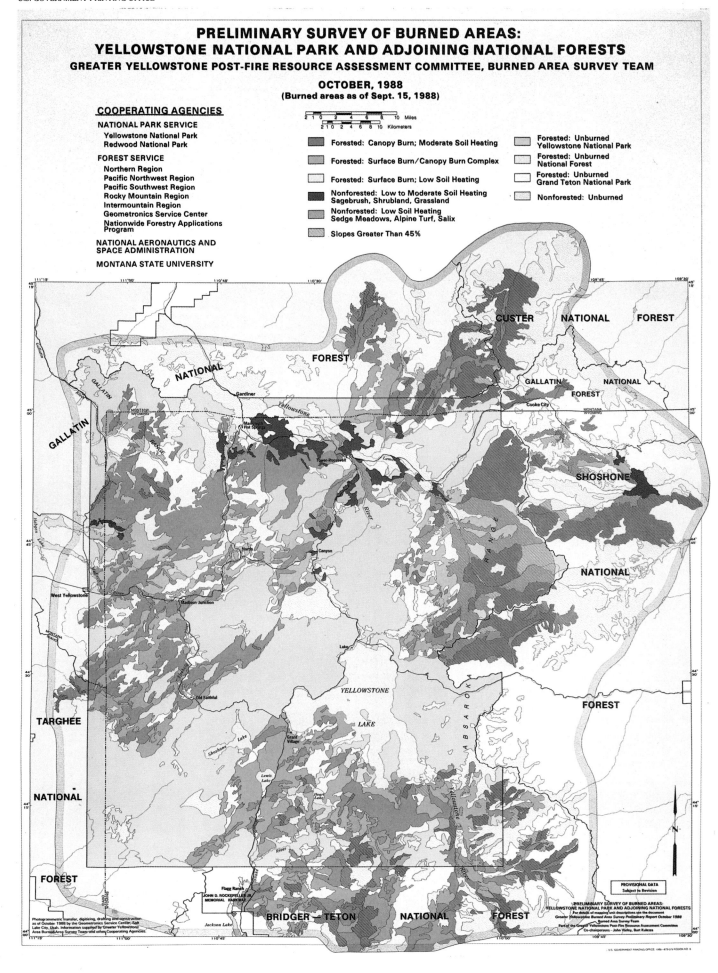

The 13 major fires that created a mosaic of blackened timber through Yellowstone in 1988 burned about 988,925 acres.

Smoke from the Wolf Lake Fire casts an eerie spell over the Lamar Valley.

could have been snuffed out in its earliest stages. But their reports indicated that another blaze, which almost burned the historic Old Faithful Inn and threatened West Yellowstone, was "impossible to control."

The 13 major fires that created a mosaic of blackened timber through Yellowstone National Park burned about 988,925 acres, more than half of which involved canopy, or the tops of trees. More than 426,575 acres involved surface area: meadow, sage and grassland.

New figures, based on satellite pictures, indicated in early winter 1988 that about 44.5 percent of the 2.2-million-acre park burned.

Henry Shovic, Burned Area Survey Team Leader, said in late 1988 that a more detailed assessment might find that as much as 15 percent of the area counted as "burned" may not have been affected by the fires.

With the exception of the North Fork Fire, which was started by careless smoking, the Hellroaring Fire and the Huck Fires, which started when a tree fell across a power line, the fires in Yellowstone were started by dry lightning.

Fire is a natural part of the ecosystem of any forest, but only five of the 13 major fires that burned in Yellowstone in 1988 were initially allowed to burn under a policy designed to use fires as a means of forest regeneration.

Reports released by Park Service and

Forest Service investigators found that decisions stemmed in part from bad information about how fast the fires could spread in the worst drought since the Dust Bowl days of the 1930s.

According to interagency review teams, Yellowstone firefighters missed an early opportunity to stop the Clover-Mist Fire in the northeastern corner of the park, which threatened Cooke City and Silver Gate down the road, by underestimating drought conditions of that summer.

Instead of using their own observations, the report found, park and national forest officials relied too much on the park's fire history and fire information gathered in the 1970s when they made early decisions about how to fight the fires.

"Historic data and perceptions indicated that a 'large fire' was around 10,000 acres," said the report on the Clover-Mist Fire. The report also said that the park manager's worst-case scenario had assumed a fire spreading to 40,000 acres. As it turned out, the Clover-Mist Fire spread to 309,600 acres.

When the Clover-Mist Fire broke out in early July, according to reports prepared by National Park Service and U.S. Forest Service fire specialists who interviewed managers and fire bosses, the park could have suppressed both fires with initial action forces, but projected spread and worst-case analysis underesti-

mated the potential of these fires to cross the Continental Divide onto the Shoshone National Forest.

Dick Hodge, a ranger from Clearwater National Forest and a member of the interagency investigating team, said that the first five days, July 9 to 14, were the only time when park officials had a chance to stop the fire.

"After that," said Hodge, "it [Clover-Mist] had grown big enough that we doubted they could have controlled it completely."

"We're mortals," said Dan Sholly, Yellowstone's chief ranger, who blamed recorded weather trends of rains in July and August that led park officials to underestimate fire conditions. But Sholly noted that even the country's best fire experts underestimated fire conditions later in the summer.

Forester Jeff Bailey, who helped perform the post-mortem on the Clover-Mist Fire, said, "They [National Park Service] wouldn't let us [U.S. Forest Service] aggressively fight the fire." Bailey said not being able to use large backburns enabled the fires to reach tinder-dry fuels and quickly get out of hand.

The Clover and the Mist fires started July 9 and July 11, respectively, eventually merging July 22. The report said the Clover and Mist fires "could have been suppressed" at minor expense in early July, if park managers had mounted a major suppression effort, but full fire-fighting efforts didn't begin until July 21, when the fires were beyond control.

The Clover-Mist Fire continued to burn until October when snow snuffed it out. Mother Nature finally did what man, after spending $23 million, could not do.

After reviewing four of the major 1988 fires that covered about half of Yellowstone National Park, teams of forest experts determined that the "natural-fire" (often called "Let-Burn") policy, allowing natural fires to burn themselves out unless they threaten humans or property, should stand—with only minor changes to improve communications.

Among the weaknesses identified by the reviews were a lack of uniform definitions for terms and a need for improved coordination of fire management directions among the various forests and parks with shared boundaries.

Jack Neckels, deputy director of the Rocky Mountain region of the National Park Service, said the latter problem had been identified in 1987 as a priority for improvement, but had not been resolved before fires broke out in, and on several sides of, the park.

Another problem that needed ad-

WILLIAM R. SALLAZ

dressing was establishing specific limits on factors such as weather, the effects of drought, and the number of fires to allow within a park. In other words, at what point officials should say "whoa!"

The teams that looked at the fires from pre-season indicators through containment also found that no wholesale changes in fire policy were required, but Neckels admitted that mistakes had been made. Some things should have been done differently. But "for the most part, actions were sound, decisions were sound," said Neckels.

More than 249 fires were identified in Yellowstone National Park in 1988, twice the normal number, making that year the worst fire season on record since 1910, when wildfires in western Montana and the Idaho panhandle destroyed more than 5 million acres—3 million in one 48-hour period. Those fires, which eventually burned themselves out, had killed 85 people and destroyed several towns. The

fires in 1910 caused people in the West to wake up and take steps to suppress forest fires.

At one point, almost 9,700 firefighters, half from the Army and Marine Corps, concentrated on 13 major fires that were identified as the most dangerous, including the one that threatened Old Faithful and another that forced the evacuation of the communities of Silver Gate and Cooke City in Montana. Over the course of the summer, 25,000 firefighters in total saw duty in Yellowstone.

High altitude assault

COURTESY OF NASA

The day before a firestorm raced across the southern flank of Old Faithful, Ron Williams flew over the area at 65,000 feet in an enhanced version of the U-2 spy plane.

Infrared and thermal sensors aboard the sophisticated aircraft were photographing the advancing North Fork Fire front. The high-altitude mission was part of a fledgling program shared by the National Aeronautics and Space Administration (NASA) and the National Park Service, a program known as "One World from Two Perspectives."

When fires began to ravage the landscape at Yellowstone, Chief Naturalist George Robinson called NASA to ask if the space agency could provide some high-altitude satellite photographs of the fires for exhibits he was putting together.

NASA not only programmed the LANDSAT-4 Earth Resource Satellite Scanner System to make a camera-run over the park, but also directed its High Altitude Aircraft Program at Ames Research Center in California to schedule ER-2 and C-130B infrared thermal mapping missions to aid fire control efforts. NASA high-altitude aircraft, the U-2 and ER-2, obtain detailed digital and photographic information about the earth's surface using an advanced multi-spectral scanner system and an array of high-resolution camera configurations. These instruments have proven more accurate and cost-effective for large-scale data collection than traditional ground methods and are being used increasingly as land-management tools.

The medium-altitude C-130 and the high-altitude ER-2 were equipped with remote sensors that could see through the layers of smoke that blanketed the entire region from early July until late September when rain and snow began to fall.

A total of six ER-2 missions were flown over Yellowstone National Park, on September 2, 6, 9, 15 and 29, with a final mission on October 6. After that time moisture in the air essentially "poked out the eyes" of the remote sensors.

Data analyst Jeff Myers at the Ames Research Center said infrared scanners can cut through dense smoke, providing there is no moisture in the smoke. Water vapor apparently acts as a shield against infrared penetration.

Myers, who scrolled through more than 12 continuous hours of videotape, said data reduction systems and high-resolution television monitors based at the Greater Yellowstone Area Unified Command in West Yellowstone, Montana

NASA EARTH SURVEY 2

NASA
707

Above: *NASA's C-130 aircraft deployed to Idaho Falls during the Yellowstone fires to collect thermal imagery that was used to map fire strategy in the park.* **Left:** *The interior of NASA's C-130 aircraft. Thermal imagery collected by scanners on board and displayed on television monitors was recorded on videotape and beamed to Area Command at West Yellowstone for distribution to field commanders.*

Facing page: *High-altitude shot of fire front advancing toward Old Faithful, shot from 65,000 feet by NASA's ER-2, an enhanced version of the U-2 spy plane. White areas are active flame fronts, red areas are superheated soils behind the flames. Line running north to south is actual park boundary. Town of West Yellowstone is halfway up the boundary line on left side of photo.*

provided fire officials with valuable "real time" images of new fires and the advancing fire front.

"With a downlink from our C-130 and ER-2," said Myers, "we were able to spot five or six wildfires in the back country of Yellowstone, fires local fire commanders didn't know existed until our pilots radioed their coordinates to the fire control center."

The September 6 mission for Chief Pilot Ron Williams began with a weather briefing in Topeka, Kansas, where one of NASA's ER-2s was on assignment.

Williams, who flew 250 missions in F-4 Phantoms for the Air Force in Cam Ranh Bay, South Vietnam, said he prepared his body by breathing 100 percent pure oxy-

gen for one hour prior to takeoff. The oxygen purged his system of nitrogen that could cause "bends," what a deep-sea diver experiences if he surfaces too quickly.

In order to arrive over the target at about noon Mountain Time to take advantage of sun angles for highest resolution, takeoff from Topeka was adjusted to allow for the 90-minute subsonic flight.

"It takes twenty to thirty minutes to get to our cruising altitude of seventy thousand feet," said Williams as he recalled his flight on the day before a firestorm threatened Old Faithful. "I could see the smoke from one hundred to one hundred fifty miles out, but you couldn't see terrain features for all of the smoke."

17

NASA's contribution to fire-fighting efforts was to give "real time" information about fire locations, sizes and intensities.

A Landsat satellite image from 525 miles altitude shows the entire state of Wyoming (black rectangle) and the smoke billowing eastward from fires in Yellowstone and in Montana's Absaroka-Beartooth Wilderness Area just north of the park.

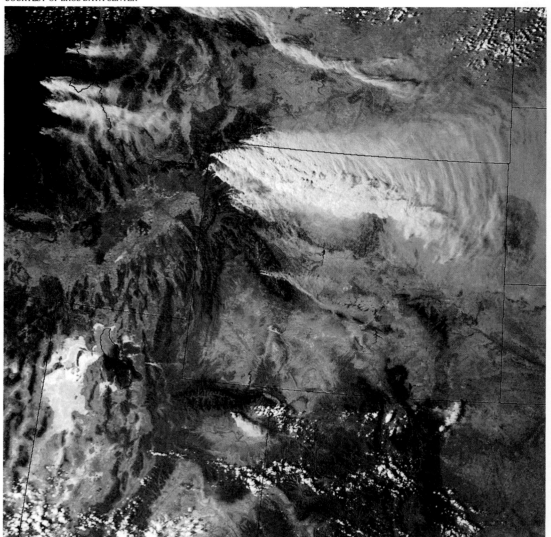

The only time Williams, and other pilots who flew the high-altitude missions, could pick out features such as rivers and lakes was when they were upwind of the fires.

It took Williams about two hours to completely photograph the 4,000-square-mile park. During that time, his aircraft made at least 12 passes at an altitude of 65,000 feet, the optimum altitude for the electronic scanners. The scanning area measures 15.4 kilometers wide by 25 meters deep. On those flight paths, the ER-2, flying at about 400 knots, recorded energy from 11 wavelength bands of visible, infrared and thermal spectra.

The detailed spectra data was converted to a video signal on the ER-2, transmitted to the downlink's ground receiver, computer-enhanced, and displayed on high-resolution television screens in the fire control center in West Yellowstone.

A three-man NASA team at the ground station also transcribed the thermal data onto topographical maps for firefighting teams. NASA Project Manager James Brass said video recordings of the overflights also were made available to strategy sessions.

The fires at Yellowstone were a learning experience for Brass and company. For example, LANDSAT gave them the "Big Picture," while the ER-2, flying at 65,000 feet, and C-130, flying at 20,000 to 25,000 feet, recorded higher-resolution information on particular fires in the park.

Unlike the ER-2, which barely has enough room in the cockpit for the pilot, the "Herc," as the C-130 is affectionately known, was large enough to accommodate U.S. Forest Service personnel who sat at specially-equipped consoles aboard the aircraft and interpreted the aerial mapping as the plane passed over fires burning below.

Like Chief Pilot Ron Williams, Doyle Krumrey, another pilot, was able to see smoke from more than 100 miles away—"somewhere east of Pocatello, Idaho"—said Krumrey, who flew U-2 spy missions over North Vietnam, Cambodia and Laos during the Vietnam War. "But from 65,000 feet the green timber looked brown and it was difficult to see ground features because of haze and dust being kicked up by the fires," said Krumrey.

Although precious time was lost when

High-flying ER-2, an enhanced version of the famous U-2 spy plane, can photograph fires from 68,000 feet through thick cloud cover with its assortment of infrared thermal cameras.

Above: *Thermal imagery collected by NASA's ER-2 at 65,000 feet over park headquarters at Mammoth. White areas represent active firefronts, red areas are super-heated soils, tan and green areas are ash layers. Large white area represents a crown fire where the tops of trees are exploding in flames. Small, thin white areas are firelines.*

Above left: *NOAA (National Oceanic and Atmospheric Administration) satellite photo covering the Greater Yellowstone Area. Seen here, an area 350 miles north and south, by 250 miles east and west. This photo, shot from 800 miles high, shows the regional effects of the Yellowstone fires. Bozeman, Montana is the approximate center of photo.*

data from early ER-2 flights from Kansas had to be analyzed at Ames Research Center in California before being sent to Yellowstone National Park, Project Manager Brass believed his people made a significant contribution to firefighting efforts, especially when the ER-2's downlink capability became operational in mid-September at West Yellowstone, and fire managers had a "real time" flow of information about location, size, rate of spread and intensity of fires they were fighting.

Like modern warfare, the fires at Yellowstone that summer were fought both in the air and on the ground.

19

Chronology of a catastrophe

MICHAEL & BARBARA PFLAUM

Not since 1910, when forest fires destroyed more than 5 million acres in Montana and Idaho, have wildfires raced across the Greater Yellowstone Area (Yellowstone and Grand Teton national parks and adjoining national forests) with such uncontrolled fury as they did in 1988.

Before being snuffed out by late October's snow, the fires burned 1,405,775 acres in Greater Yellowstone, an area almost the size of the state of Delaware.

The summer of 1988 was the driest on record in Yellowstone. Practically no rain fell in June, July or August, an event previously unrecorded in the park's 112-year written record of weather conditions.

Since 1931, lightning has been the cause of an average of 72 fires per year in Yellowstone. Since 1972, there have been 235 naturally-caused fires in the park, which have burned an average of 240 acres each.

By early summer in 1988, about 20 lightning-caused fires were burning. According to the Yellowstone Fire Plan, fires were evaluated on a case-by-case basis before being allowed to burn.

But by mid-July it was obvious to park officials that Mother Nature was not playing by the rules. On July 15, the fires had consumed about 8,600 acres. After that day, no new natural fires were allowed to burn. After July 21, all fires were subjected to full suppression.

On July 27, during a visit to Yellowstone, the Secretary of the Interior stated that the "natural-fire" policy had been suspended, but the horse was already out of the barn.

Accepted firefighting techniques—such as constructing fire lines along the edges of advancing fire to create fuel-free buffer zones, and backfiring to reduce fuel buildups in the face of advancing fires—frequently were ineffective because high winds caused the fires to spot, a phenomenon by which wind carries burning embers from the tops of 200-foot flames well ahead of the main fire.

Spotting up to a mile and a half distant made even the widest bulldozer lines useless and enabled fires to jump usually-helpful barriers such as roads and rivers.

The frustration of firefighters facing these kinds of field conditions was summed up by Denny Bungarz, a U.S. Forest Service fireboss from Mendocino National Forest in California. Bungarz, the Incident Commander on the North Fork Fire that threatened Old Faithful, said, "We threw everything we had at that fire from Day One. We tried everything we

MICHAEL H. FRANCIS

A number of major fires started outside the park and moved in. It was as if Mother Nature had placed a flaming noose around Yellowstone Park and tightened it daily.

Sunset through a smoky haze in Yellowstone.

Facing page: *One of millions of trees that became flaming torches in Yellowstone during the fires of 1988.*

knew of, or could think of, and that fire kicked our ass from one end of the park to the other."

A number of major fires—most notably the North Fork, Hellroaring, Storm Creek, Huck and Mink Creek—started outside the park and moved in. It was as if Mother Nature had placed a flaming noose around Yellowstone Park and tightened it daily.

Following, in order of ignition, is a chronology of Yellowstone's fires in 1988.

JUNE 14

Lightning starts a fire in the Custer National Forest north of the Northeast Entrance to Yellowstone National Park. The Storm Creek Fire, as this one was called, began in the rugged Absaroka-Beartooth Wilderness and eventually grew to more than 95,000 acres and threatened two gateway communities.

Fire Behavior Specialist Larry Vanderlin, assigned to the Storm Creek Fire, said the extreme lack of moisture during the summer of 1988 wrote a new chapter in fire behavior textbooks.

At least six dry cold fronts crossed the Greater Yellowstone Area in the summer, producing winds up to 60 miles per hour. These winds sometimes drove fires five to 10 miles per day. Forest fires, even the fiercest ones, have a tendency to "lie down" or die down during the night when winds subside, but not that summer. There often was fierce burning at night and, for that reason, no firefighters were sent into the timber after dark.

If contending with Mother Nature's fickleness wasn't enough, firefighters also had to contend with some of her children. Buffalo became a problem at the Storm Creek Fire camp outside Cooke City when they rubbed against helicopters. To prevent further damage by the bison, a fence was built around the helipad.

A helicopter was grounded at Mammoth Hot Springs when a bull elk decided to rub the velvet off his antlers on the fiberglass air intake of an engine on a chopper, and punctured it.

A hand crew building a fire line in Hayden Valley in late August was watched by a grizzly bear about 100 yards away. Fearing for their safety, firefighters called in a helicopter that scared away the bear.

Grizzly bears forced the closing of several spike camps near Silver Gate and Cooke City, but the real problem there was a backburn. It caused someone to add a "d" to the sign outside Cooke City: Cooked City.

That backburn was to reduce fuel in front of the Storm Creek Fire, thereby keeping it from sweeping down the Soda Butte Canyon and incinerating the two towns. Fire Behavior Analyst Rod Norum said officials knew the backburn would not stop the fire, but they hoped it would save the towns (which it did) by keeping the main fire on the north side of town. Without the backburn, Norum said, the fire front would have been sucked down the deep canyon walls, pushed by a dry cold front with high winds.

21

With the exception of three fires, most of the blazes in Yellowstone were ignited by dry lightning strikes like this one.

JUNE 23

A bolt of lightning strikes near the remote Shoshone Lake about 10 miles southwest of Grant Village. When the fire first was reported, it involved about 70 acres. But the fire grew rapidly. In just more than one month, the Red-Shoshone Fire, as the first blaze inside the park later would be called, grew to more than 19,000 acres and forced the evacuation of 3,000 visitors and employees at Grant Village on July 23.

JUNE 25

Two days after the Shoshone Fire broke out in the south-central part of the park, lightning started the Fan Fire in the extreme northwestern corner of the park along Highway 191 about 31 miles north of the West Entrance.

JULY 1

Lightning starts a fire on the southwest side of Lewis Lake a few miles south of Shoshone Lake. When first reported, the fire had consumed about 680 acres.

The Falls Fire is started by lightning just east of the South Entrance to Yellowstone. What was discovered as a 25-acre fire grew to 3,728 acres by August 24, when the Falls Fire crossed the South Entrance Road en route to merge with the Red-Shoshone Fire.

JULY 5

Lightning ignites the Lava Fire in the northern end of the park halfway between Park Headquarters at Mammoth Hot Springs and Roosevelt Lodge. The fire involved less than one acre when first reported.

JULY 9

The Mist Fire is started by a dry-lightning strike in the extreme eastern part of the park near the Lamar River. The size of the fire was only 200 acres when it was first reported.

JULY 11

Four fires break out: Raven, southwest of the Mist Fire; Clover, just north of Mist; Lovely, between Mist and Raven; and Mink, outside the south boundary of the park.

The Raven Fire grew to almost 60 acres by July 29, before burning itself out.

The Clover Fire broke out on the Mirror Plateau in the northeast corner of the park when lightning ignited dry tinder.

There were three major advances during the life of the Clover-Mist Fire: July 23, when it reached the Shoshone National Forest for the first time; August 20, when the fire again crossed the Continental Divide onto the Shoshone National Forest; and on September 6, when it burned homes and timber in Crandall Creek and 40,000 acres in Jones Creek in the North Absaroka Wilderness.

Four residences, one store and 14 mobile homes were destroyed in the Crandall area, but no lives were lost. Injuries also were kept to a minimum among firefighters. More than 872,000 work-hours were expended on the Clover-Mist Fire; however, most of the 275 documented injuries were in the twisted-ankle category. Despite rugged terrain, the injury frequency rate was one third of the normal injury rate in forest fire suppression.

The Clover-Mist Fire destroyed an estimated 12.5 billion board feet of timber in the Shoshone National Forest, a substantial portion of the forest's suitable timber base. A post-fire inspection of the burned timber indicated that only 1,000 acres could be sold at a "fire sale." Bids were accepted on trees whose bark was burned, but whose wood still was usable for products such as plywood.

From an economic point of view, Don G. Despain, research biologist and plant ecologist at Yellowstone, told the New York *Times,* "Dead trees may be a loss to home builders," but from an ecological point of view, "dead trees are not a loss to woodpeckers who live in them."

At the height of the Clover-Mist Fire, firefighters numbered 1,700 (which included 660 U.S. Army personnel) and equipment totaled three helicopters and 60 fire engines.

A review of the Clover-Mist Fire revealed one glaring error: Forest Service and Park Service managers failed to recognize the full potential for a severe fire season. Severe burning conditions increased the fire size by 45,000 acres on August 20, resulting in spotting and further fire spread onto the Shoshone National Forest.

A review panel concluded that the Clover and Mist fires could have been controlled as late as July 14 had severe conditions been recognized. The number of strategic options decreased from "confine, contain and control" on July 14 to "confine and partial containment" on July 23. Failure to recognize extreme drought conditions contributed to the cost of suppression: $23 million for the Clover-Mist Fire.

At times there was confusion as to who was in charge of the Clover-Mist Fire. This confusion led to disagreements over tactical decisions.

A total of three requests were made between August 28 and September 10 to

As a bulldozer gouges a fireline through some sagebrush, a twin-engine bomber is preparing to drop retardant on a nearby fire.

use bulldozers on the south end of the Clover-Mist Fire. Line officers wanted to build dozer lines along the Pelican Creek Drainage, up Cub Creek and from Turbid Lake to Jones Pass, but the first two requests were denied by Park Superintendent Robert Barbee.

The third request was given the "go ahead" if the incident commander believed that it was absolutely necessary in order to stop the fire. As it turned out, snow fell the following day, and the request was dropped by the commander.

Miscommunications between park headquarters and the East Entrance resulted in fire crews being denied access to Yellowstone on September 8 and 10. During this period, the gate was closed to the public coming from Cody, Wyoming and personnel on the gate apparently interpreted the order to mean firefighters as well. However, the delays at the gate did not affect the outcome of the Clover-Mist Fire, according to an official investigation.

There also were logistical snafus. Supplies sent to the fire base at Crandall, Wyoming were appropriated by other camps while en route, and never arrived at the Clover-Mist Fire. Aerial retardant was not received when requested.

While fire managers tried to re-establish lines of communications and untangle supply lines on the Clover-Mist Fire, a fourth major fire broke out.

The Mink Fire is started by lightning in the Teton Wilderness, Bridger-Teton National Forest, in the extreme southeastern corner of the park. When first reported, the fire had burned only 4,000 acres.

On July 22, 1988, careless cigarette smoking started the North Fork Fire, which would threaten Old Faithful and make front-page headlines for weeks.

The rate of spread of Yellowstone fires between July 16 and September 16, 1988.

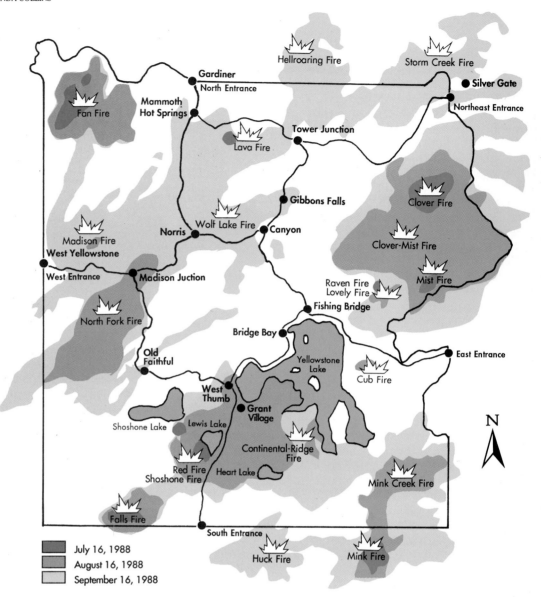

July 16, 1988
August 16, 1988
September 16, 1988

Yellowstone Fires

July 16 to September 16, 1988

JULY 21

The Clover and Mist fires are declared wildfires when they threaten the Shoshone National Forest. Up to this date these two fires, along with three other lightning-caused fires, had been allowed to burn.

JULY 22

The Clover and Mist fires merge. At this point they had burned 10,700 and 1,527 acres respectively. Until this date, all of the fires inside the park had been blamed on lightning. But on this day, four loggers allegedly started a fire that would ignite the whole western side of the park and make front-page headlines and gain

coverage on the nightly news on television.

The North Fork Fire began outside the park in the Targhee National Forest in Idaho when four men cutting firewood took a smoke break. An investigation revealed that the men dropped lighted cigarette butts into some dry underbrush. Within hours, the fire became a raging inferno.

Under federal law, people who start forest fires can be liable for damage and suppression costs, which totaled about $25 million for the North Fork Fire. However, in this case, the loggers were charged only with petty offenses: dropping lighted cigarettes and littering. Conviction could mean six months in jail or a $500 fine or both.

Chuck Burns, a Forest Service special agent on the Targhee, said there was no evidence of deliberate arson.

It took some backwoods detective work to find the loggers. Firefighters who arrived on the scene followed the blaze upwind to find its point of origin. They found numerous butts of a generic brand of cigarette scattered on the ground, a brand sold on the nearby Fort Hunt Indian Reservation.

A check of the Forest Service registry turned up names of people who signed up for logging on July 22, the day the fire began. Confronted with the evidence, the four loggers admitted smoking the generic brand of cigarettes, but the damage had been done.

The ignition point was about 300 yards from the Yellowstone National Park boundary. It didn't take long for the grass fire to spread quickly to dense stands of lodgepole pine that had been killed by bark beetles.

A Forest Service employee spotted the fire and sounded the alarm at about 2:30 P.M. Shortly after the initial report, Rodd Richardson, District Ranger on the Island Park District of the Targhee National Forest, could see a smoke column from his office about 15 miles away.

"It was really ripping," said Richardson, who immediately requested smokejumpers and a strike team of engines, dozers and hand crews.

Smokejumpers from West Yellowstone reached the fire first at about 2:50 P.M., but high winds caused their aircraft, *Empire II,* to abort the mission. As they circled the fire in their jump plane, the smokejumpers estimated the fire size at about 75 acres.

According to the Incident Status Summary filed six hours later, the fire had grown to 460 acres. By then 62 people were assigned to fight it.

Suppression forces in the initial attack included three engines, a 15-person Forest Service hand crew, two dozers and four airtanker loads of retardant. The airtankers concentrated on the flanks of the fire, but Richardson did not believe the tankers were effective.

Spot fires were observed as much as one half mile in front of the main fire by the lead plane pilot, who set up the angle of attack for the airtankers. Strong gusty wind and falling snags made suppression efforts extremely dangerous for ground personnel.

By the time initial attack forces reached the fire, it already had spread into Yellowstone National Park. Although

Joe Evans, West Yellowstone District Ranger, requested that a full suppression strategy be used on the fire inside the park, he denied Richardson's request to use dozers within the park for initial attack.

Due to a drop in the wind's velocity after dark, and to gentle terrain, Richardson, the Initial Attack Incident Commander, believed a dozer line could have been built around the main fire on the first night, July 22.

JULY 23

After Area Commander Troy Kurth and Chief Ranger Dan Sholly made a helicopter reconnaissance of the fire, Kurth stated that dozer lines could have been built around the main fire in Yellowstone, but it was his judgment that dozer lines probably could not have held and, due to the extreme fire behavior, there could have been loss of equipment, crews in danger and unnecessary damage to the environment.

"The end result," said Kurth, "would have been the same. An escaped fire."

A post-fire investigation by a team of interagency fire experts found that at this point in the Yellowstone fire scenario, the North Fork Fire was a lower priority than other fires in the park.

On July 23, when the North Fork Fire just was getting started, Grant Village was being evacuated. Larry Whelan, operations section chief, concentrated his limited resources along utility corridors. Whelan said it costs $1 million a mile to replace power lines.

JULY 24

The North Fork Fire made a major run, growing to 2,500 acres and racing to within six miles of Old Faithful. Area Commander Troy Kurth reported 150-foot

Piles of pulaskis, double-headed firefighting tools invented by a veteran firefighter, waiting to be picked up at one of seven major fire camps in Yellowstone.

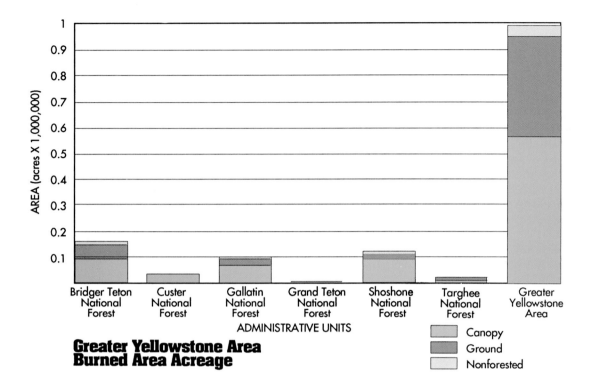

**Greater Yellowstone Area
Burned Area Acreage**

flames flashing in the smoke column. For more than two months adverse weather, dry fuels, lack of adequate resources, the size of the fire, its rapid growth and safety concerns kept the North Fork Fire from being controlled.

Despite extremely dry conditions, an official investigation found that the early suppression decisions on the North Fork Fire were "consistent" with policy and overall needs within the Greater Yellowstone Area considering the available resources, the pressing needs for them on other fires, fire conditions throughout the area, the probability of controlling the fire and the safety of firefighters.

Looking back on a fire that was driven by 20-mile-per-hour winds, Keith Burch, Fire Management Office on the Targhee National Forest, said there was no way to tell if dozers would have made a difference on a fire that was spotting a half mile ahead.

"No one will ever know," said Burch. "Once the fire crossed the boundary line, it was their [National Park Service] fire."

Because of the way the North Fork fire started, it was the most controversial of 13 major fires that ravaged Yellowstone from June until October's snowfall.

JULY 27

The North Fork Fire grows to 9,700 acres as 1,000 firefighters try desperately to contain it. The Clover-Mist Fire has grown to 46,825 acres as 100 firefighters work to stop further spread into the timber-rich Shoshone National Forest.

JULY 29

The Clover-Mist Fire has grown to 68,035 acres. Two hundred thirty-eight firefighters now are trying to stop it from spreading further.

AUGUST 2

The Clover-Mist Fire has grown to 73,754 acres, including 1,175 acres in the Shoshone National Forest. The North Fork Fire has grown to 17,700 acres, almost doubling in size in the past week. One thousand firefighters now are committed to this fire. Under federal law, the careless smokers who threw lighted cigarette butts into some grass on the Targhee National Forest could be held liable, if convicted, for all of the government's cost of fighting the North Fork Fire: about $25 million.

AUGUST 5

The Fan Fire, which has burned 16,600 acres in the northwestern corner of the park, is being contained within park boundaries. The Lava Fire, which began July 5, is contained. The Lovely Fire is being monitored.

MICHAEL & BARBARA PFLAUM

Bull elk grazing in a meadow as the timber behind him goes up in flames. Somehow, life goes on for wildlife. Most animals simply moved out of the way of advancing fires.

AUGUST 10

The 20,800-acre Red Fire joins the 25,200-acre Shoshone Fire to become the Red-Shoshone Fire in the southern part of the park. The Clover-Mist Fire has grown to 81,769 acres in the northeastern part of the park. More than 1,500 firefighters are committed to the Fan Fire. The Mink Creek Fire that has consumed almost 8,000 acres in Yellowstone and 22,000 acres in Teton Wilderness is moving south. The North Fork Fire has grown to 31,650 acres and has closed Firehole Canyon Drive. The Shallow Fire that was discovered July 31 has burned into the Clover-Mist Fire. The Lava Fire is contained.

AUGUST 14

The Clover-Mist Fire has grown to 94,724 acres as the Shallow and Fern fires burn into the Clover-Mist. The North Fork Fire has grown to 52,960, the Red-Shoshone to 55,000 acres.

AUGUST 15

Carelessness at an outfitter's camp near Gardiner, Montana is believed responsible for a fire that grows rapidly into an 81,900-acre blaze known as the Hell-roaring Fire, but lack of sufficient infrared equipment, aircraft and personnel hampered suppression of this fire.

The lack of proper communications equipment resulted in problems with dropping the right supplies to the right locations in the wilderness and in coordinating trash pickups at spike camps where firefighters bivouacked whenever the distance from base camp to the fire became excessive.

The lack of regular trash pickups may not present too much of a problem if you live in suburbia, but in the wilderness, grizzly bears raid spike camps when garbage is not picked up on a regular basis. And bears were a problem in the summer of 1988.

AUGUST 20

Fed by drought conditions and high winds, fires consumed a record 150,000 acres on August 20—a day that went down in Yellowstone history as "Black Saturday"—but only a single building was lost at Grant Village: an outhouse.

AUGUST 21

High winds cause flareups around Grant Village and West Thumb. The Huck Fire starts outside the park near the South Entrance when a tree falls across a powerline south of Flagg Ranch, causing the closure of the John D. Rockefeller, Jr. Memorial Highway linking Grand Teton and Yellowstone national parks.

AUGUST 22

The Clover-Mist Fire has swelled to 156,502 acres and now threatens Silver Gate and Cooke City, two communities outside the Northeast Entrance to the park. U.S. Army troops from Fort Lewis, Washington arrive to give civilian firefighters a break. Fire trucks and crews are stationed in Silver Gate and Cooke City to protect property.

The North Fork Fire has grown to 91,700 acres.

AUGUST 24

The North Fork Fire increases its size another 5,000 acres overnight and has grown so large that fire officials add a second commander to coordinate attacks on the northern flank of the fire, the Wolf Lake Fire. Together, these fires eventually burned 504,025 acres. Hellroaring Fire has consumed 33,000 acres outside the park as it burned to the northeast. The Storm Creek Fire, which began June 14, has burned 25,000 acres, but still is located in the Custer National Forest north of Cooke City—currently not a problem to Silver Gate or Cooke City. The Huck Fire, which

U.S. Army soldiers preparing to leave camp for a day of fighting fires in the nearby mountains. The canvas pouches on their hips contain one-man fire shelters to be deployed as a last resort.

began three days ago, has spread to 6,000 acres.

AUGUST 26

Fire officials lump all of the fires in the southern end of the park into one: the 172,025-acre Snake River Complex.

AUGUST 28

More than 1,700 firefighters—including infantry and 56 civilian crews, with 13 engines, six dozers and three helicopters—are committed to the Clover-Mist Fire that has increased in size to 182,100 acres. Additional manpower is being committed to the Hellroaring and Storm Creek fires.

SEPTEMBER 1

Seven strike teams of infantry are supporting civilian personnel on the North Fork Fire, where 1,058 firefighters, 26 engines, eight dozers, 24 hand crews and seven helicopters are committed to battle. The North Fork Fire has burned more than 109,000 acres. The Clover-Mist Fire has burned more than 231,000 acres. The Snake River Complex—which includes the Red-Shoshone, Falls and Mink fires—has blackened 156,150 acres. The Hellroaring Fire, at 45,000 acres, is four

miles from the Storm Creek Fire, which has consumed 41,000 acres. They are expected to burn together.

SEPTEMBER 4

As a precaution, all non-essential fire personnel and residents are ordered to leave Silver Gate and Cooke City.

SEPTEMBER 5

Evacuation of Silver Gate and Cooke City completed. A spot fire has moved just north of Silver Gate. The main fire also is within one mile of Cooke City.

SEPTEMBER 6

The Hellroaring Fire joins the Storm Creek Fire. A backfire will be set to protect Silver Gate and Cooke City.

SEPTEMBER 7

The North Fork Fire has spotted to within three fourths of a mile of the Old Faithful area. Tourists and non-essential personnel were evacuated. Sprinklers were installed at the Montana Power substation and along utility corridors. Late in the afternoon, a firestorm swept across the southern end of the Old Faithful complex destroying 16 tourist and employee cabins as well as a barn used as a vehicle storage shed. The Old Faithful Inn was not touched.

The Huck burns into the Falls Fire, exhibiting erratic, dangerous behavior.

SEPTEMBER 8

The spot fire that burned north of Silver Gate passed Cooke Pass east of Cooke City. One outbuilding near town and three isolated cabins were burned.

The Wolf Lake Fire burns to within three feet of some Canyon Village buildings. West-southwest winds were expected to push the fire toward Lamar Valley.

SEPTEMBER 9

The Clover-Mist Fire, now at 304,100 acres, destroys 20 buildings, trailers and sheds in the Crandall Creek area. The Fan Fire now is contained.

SEPTEMBER 10

The Huck Fire has burned to within one mile of the Mink Fire. The Clover-Mist fire jumped the road where the Storm Creek Incident Command Post was located. Rain fell in the Snake River Complex, enough to form puddles. Weather forecasters were predicting snow.

SEPTEMBER 11

Snow falls over much of Yellowstone National Park, slowing the spread of the

The melting of September's first snow caused seeds scattered by the fires to germinate in the ash and send forth tender shoots of green grass.

A Park Service sign about the danger of forest fires fell victim along the road from Norris to Canyon.

Clover-Mist, Snake River Complex and North Fork fires.

SEPTEMBER 12

The Huck and Mink fires merge. The Huck-Mink Complex, as the fire now is called, involved an estimated 67,175 acres within Yellowstone National Park and an estimated 157,650 acres within the Bridger-Teton National Forest.

SEPTEMBER 13

Two battalions of Marines arrive at West Yellowstone Airport. The 1st Battalion, 3rd Marine Division and 1st Battalion, 5th Marine Division bivouac at Madison Campground. It rained all day over much of the park.

SEPTEMBER 15

The Huck-Mink Complex, which burned 225,500 acres, is 100 percent contained; however, there is no estimated date of control. It cost about $10 million to suppress the fire.

SEPTEMBER 19

The Clover-Mist Fire, which has burned 411,500 acres, is 70 percent contained, but the Storm Creek Fire (which consumed 107,847 acres), the Hellroaring Fire (which burned 81,950 acres) and the Snake River Complex (which burned 224,000 acres) are 100 percent contained.

SEPTEMBER 26

The Clover-Mist Fire is 83 percent contained; however, the North Fork Fire (which has burned more than 400,000 acres to date) is only 50 percent contained—with total containment not expected until mid-October. The Clover-Mist Fire was second only to the North Fork Fire in terms of total acreage burned: 319,575 vs. 504,025 acres, respectively.

END OF FIRE SEASON

The degree of damage varied substantially from fire to fire in Yellowstone. For example, park studies found about 30 percent of the area within the Fan Fire in the northwest corner of the park burned, while as much as 70 percent of the Lava Creek, Firehole and Madison River areas burned.

Preliminary surveys suggest moderate soil heating; 10 percent received high heat, but only one percent received extreme heat. Light to moderate heats do not customarily kill seeds and bulbs buried more than an inch below the surface, so Yellowstone's plant communities will be fully capable of regenerating.

When Mother Nature gave Yellowstone a light dusting of snow on Sunday morning, September 11, it was as if she were saying, "Enough's enough." The snow that fell prompted local radio stations to begin playing Christmas songs, like "Jingle Bells." The melting snow provided the scorched earth with desperately-needed moisture to help seeds scattered by the fires germinate in the ash and send forth tender shoots of green grass.

This rebirth caused biologist Joe Halliday to exclaim, "Yellowstone was born of fire, and now it's being reborn."

Counting the costs

GUY R. HIGBEE

It cost the government $111,377,623 to fight fires in the Greater Yellowstone Area in the summer of 1988. That averages out to more than $1.5 million a day. A record $6 million was spent in one 24-hour period, September 9-10. Almost one third of the $111 million was spent on the North Fork Fire, making it the most expensive fire fought.

According to Lucy Nix, finance coordinator for the Greater Yellowstone Fire Command, about 43 percent of the $111 million went for firefighters' wages. About 23 percent went to air support. Items such as food, axes, pulaskis and sleeping bags amounted to 18 percent. Sixteen percent was spent on miscellaneous items.

Seventy-seven helicopters and a dozen fixed-wing aircraft flew 18,000 flight hours of close-air support. The hourly rate for renting one of those helicopters was about $1,700.

Although no firefighters lost their lives in Yellowstone National Park proper, a Bureau of Land Management employee was killed October 11 while battling a blaze in the Shoshone National Forest when a 72-foot-tall dead tree fell on him from behind.

The death of Edward Hutton, 26, of Casper, Wyoming was the second attributed directly to a blaze in the region. A falling tree also killed a firefighter near Polebridge, Montana in September.

Three people died when helicopters involved in firefighting crashed in Wyoming and Washington.

Forest fires burned almost 5 million acres throughout the West in 1988, a year federal officials have called "the worst fire season" since the turn of the century.

A field survey by the National Park Service found 256 large mammals dead within Yellowstone as a result of the fires. About 150 elk, bison, deer and bear carcasses were found outside the park on national forest land.

After an extensive survey conducted last fall before snow covered the park with a fluffy white blanket, personnel located 243 elk, four deer, four moose and five bison carcasses. No bear carcasses were found: amazing, considering that only two of the 36 radio-collared grizzly bears moved a substantial distance from the fires. Most of the grizzlies, according to Chief Naturalist George Robinson, moved out of the way long enough for the fires to pass, and then ambled back into the burned areas.

"The number of ungulate [hoofed-mammal] deaths caused by the fires is a very small percentage of total wildlife

It cost the government more than $111 million to fight 1988's fires in the Greater Yellowstone Area—more than $1.5 million per day.

Buffalo returning to their grazing area in the Lamar Valley, despite the Wolf Lake Fire that continues to burn.

Facing page: *Ursus americanus, the black bear. This particular black bear is cinnamon in color. Surprisingly few large animal carcasses, none of them bears, were found after the fires.*

populations within the park," said Superintendent Robert Barbee. Yellowstone's elk population right after the fires was estimated between 30,000 and 35,000, and bison and deer at 2,700 and 2,000, respectively.

Of the total number of animal carcasses, 213 were located within the perimeter of the human-caused North Fork Fire and probably died from smoke inhalation on Friday, September 9, when the fire front was pushed by southwesterly winds. Field personnel examined the tracheas of these mammals to help determine whether the cause of death was due to smoke or burns.

Several small animals, such as red squirrels, porcupines and birds, also were located and identified as fire-related mortalities.

No actual numbers are available to reflect the effect of fires on insects in the park, but researchers have noted variable results, depending on the type of insect. The effects on airborne insects like butterflies and bees depended on the stage of development, such as whether the insect was in larval or adult form. Surface-dwelling insects, primarily grasshoppers, crickets and surface-dwelling beetles, were more heavily impacted. Soil-dwelling insects such as ants often were not affected at all since only 22,000 acres (one percent of the park) suffered "high-intensity fires" that scorched the earth so badly it will not be able to renew itself.

Fifteen general areas were identified within the park by fire behaviorists and observers as having burned hot and fast enough to possibly affect large animals.

Park personnel were aware of only two instances when animals were humanely killed because of fire-related injuries. A badly-injured black bear estimated to be about four years of age was found near Cooke City. According to the Montana State Highway patrolman who killed the bear on September 9, its feet were severely burned.

In late October, park rangers received a report of a bull elk with severely burned hooves, and destroyed the animal near Lava Creek.

More than 700 hours were spent by field personnel conducting the survey. Approximately 263 miles were surveyed by foot and horseback, and more than 47 hours were spent in aerial search by helicopter.

Throughout the survey, numerous live animals were observed in the burned areas and in the immediate vicinity of carcasses. All carcasses were left "in-place" as field personnel observed extensive scavenging by grizzly and black bears, eagles, ravens and coyotes. Even after death, animals play an important part in the ecological system.

U.S. Fish and Wildlife Service researchers have begun studying the effects of wind-blown ash and smoke on fish and other aquatic life in high-elevation lakes. Biologists are sampling water in Montana's Gallatin and Custer national forests and Wyoming's Shoshone National Forest.

Fish and Wildlife Director Frank

Blackened lodgepole pine trunks and ash were all that was left in some areas of the Wolf Lake Fire.

Dunkle said experts think some small, isolated lakes amid high alpine tundra may show an increase in acidity, because of airborne contaminants carried by smoke. A measurable, but short-term, increase in pH and alkalinity also was expected from ash and charcoal in all extensively-burned watersheds during the first few snow-melts and runoffs. But scientists believe most fish can tolerate the short-term changes in water chemistry.

Meanwhile, another scientist is studying the effects of the fire on wildlife by analyzing urine-soaked snow to determine whether animals are getting enough to eat. Biologist Glenn DelGiudice perfected the testing, which experts think has great promise for aiding wildlife studies around the world.

"Glenn's technique is generating a great deal of excitement among researchers," said L. David Mech, a U.S. Fish and Wildlife Service scientist who is an internationally-known wolf expert. "It can be applied anywhere animals live in snow for part of the year."

Mech and Ulysses S. Seal, a biochemist widely recognized for his research on endangered wildlife, initiated the technique of using urine-soaked snow in wildlife research, but several years ago they

turned over perfection of the technique to DelGiudice, then a graduate student at the University of Minnesota.

For the past two years, DelGiudice has studied Yellowstone's elk and bison under an agreement between the Veterans Administration, for whom he works, and the National Park Service which manages the 2.2-million-acre park. His work will allow scientists to compare the health of bison and elk before and after the summer fires.

DelGiudice is among the many scientists who are preparing a plan for studying the effects of the fires. He stressed that, while the fires charred extensive timber and brush, the burned-over areas form a mosaic pattern rather than a contiguous tract.

"That's important," said DelGuidice, "because while vegetation has not yet returned to areas burned in late summer, plants already have emerged in tracts that were charred earlier." Those young plants helped bison and elk survive the following winter.

Survival of the species is the reason the Humane Society and United Animal Nations dispatched Chief Investigator Terry McKim to Yellowstone at the height of the summer fires. "Both organizations were concerned about how animals are treated during disasters like this one," said McKim.

"If you look at what happened, it's a sad situation," said McKim, "but long-term I think the fires will stimulate new growth." McKim said two and a half years after another disastrous fire, the elk herd tripled at Klamath Falls, Idaho.

But what about people in surrounding communities who say the forests will never return in their lifetimes? "This was just a moment in time," mused McKim philosophically, "and to have to wait forty or fifty years for a forest to return isn't very long when you're looking at millions of years since creation."

"It would be best if man just stepped back, and let Yellowstone heal itself," concluded McKim in her 15-page report to the United Animal Nations. But the real story of survival of the species won't be known until researchers evaluate the effect of the fires on the winter ranges of the elk and bison.

"You gotta face the fact that Mother Nature has delivered wildlife a double whammy," said wildlife biologist Greg Felzine as he sat in his pickup truck on the road between Mammoth Hot Springs and the town of Gardiner, near a sign proclaiming this spot to be on the 45th parallel, halfway between the Equator and the North Pole.

Felzine was radio-tracking some bull elk he had collared, plotting their movements as they searched for food. "Some of the bulls didn't look as healthy as they should have entering the mating season," observed Felzine, "and with the fire, it might be a bad year for the elk."

Area residents outside the park, such as businessman Hayes Kirby of Silver Gate, expected to find the bones of thousands of elk when the snow melts. "Their winter range was destroyed," said Kirby, who wanted to organize an airborne hay drop.

"We don't want a petting zoo in Yellowstone," said the former F-15 fighter pilot. "But if we don't feed them, they'll die." His idea was promptly shot down by Chief Naturalist George Robinson.

"There's no good reason, only emotional and often misguided ones, to consider a supplemental feeding program," said Robinson. Such a program, he said, could have serious ill effects on ungulates.

For example, the elk and bison in Yellowstone have no experience with feed lots. "They probably couldn't find hay dropped from airplanes in deep snow, unless the bales were dropped on top of their heads," said Robinson. And if the animals did get to the supplementary

NATURAL FIRES: A NECESSARY EVIL

"Fires are as much a part of the ecosystem as snow, wind and rain," said William H. Romme, an assistant professor of biology at Fort Lewis College in Durango, Colorado. Romme, who has studied the history of fires at Yellowstone, said a forest without fires would be a very unnatural place.

For years ecologists have argued against suppressing fires the moment they break out, because that causes all of the trees in a forest to mature at the same time, instead of having stages of growth like sculptured carpet with varying heights of fiber.

Foresters have argued that such suppression would result in an accumulation of brush and debris that, once ignited, would burn so hot and spread so fast, a forest fire would be impossible to stop. This is precisely what occurred in 1988 in Yellowstone National Park.

MICHAEL H. FRANCIS

An old bleached elk skull reminds us of the wildlife casualties in the fires. Autopsies revealed that most died of smoke inhalation; they did not burn to death.

About 80 percent of the park is covered by lodgepole pine. These large stands of pine matured more than 100 years ago, and were waiting to be torched.

A 1987 report indicated that more than 50 percent of the 12 million acres that comprise the Greater Yellowstone Area had moderate to high potential for high-intensity fires.

Two research projects have enhanced man's understanding of fire ecology at Yellowstone. A study by D.L. Taylor indicates what can be expected in stands of lodgepole pine. Taylor discovered a threefold increase in species of plants, birds and small mammals in pine that had burned 25 years earlier.

Historically, the northern Douglas-fir–steppe zone of the park has had the highest natural fire frequency of any area in Yellowstone. By cross-dating fire scars on trees being felled, D.S. Houston found 11 trees from seven different stands showing 28 different fires from 1525 to 1870.

"Fire scars are a relatively crude measure of frequency and may underestimate the past influence of fire in this ecosystem," wrote Houston in a paper on wildfires in Yellowstone Park, but Houston believes much of the area surveyed would have burned at least one to four times since the park was established in 1872 were it not for the intervention of modern man.

Philosophically speaking, biologist Joe Halliday said the 1988 fires in Yellowstone were Mother Nature's way of getting even with man for denying her access to the forest.

"None of us will see the likes of this again in our lifetime," said Don Buss, a naturalist park ranger. "The last time the park burned like this was in the 1600s," said Buss. "All this fuel has been building up ever since, and we've added to it by putting out all fires for over 100 years. The park needs this [fire], within limits, and it will be the best thing to help expand the age diversity of our forest."

JEFF VANUGA

Two weeks after the fire, new growth was spotted in the blackened forest at Norris.

feed, Robinson feels it would discourage migration outside the park to better food sources.

From a purely scientific point of view, Robinson says rumen flora of wild ungulates is not adapted to artificial foods, and the inability of those microorganisms to efficiently process artificial foods could cause increased mortality among elk and bison feeding on that food.

"There is also the danger of increased spread of disease and parasites if you concentrate animals in feeding areas," said Robinson.

Robinson believed there was plenty of winter range left for the elk in Yellowstone National Park. An in-house study conducted before snow covered the park showed that less than 10 percent of the Gibbon winter ranges and less than 25 percent of the Firehole winter ranges were burned. But more than 50 percent of the Madison, Duck and Cougar Creek winter ranges was destroyed.

The fires of 1988 also burned a significant portion of winter and summer range for three bison herds in Yellowstone and led to plans for aerial monitoring of the herds' movement over the following several years.

Preliminary reconnaissance indicates a minimum of two bald eagle nests and possibly more were directly affected by the fires. A minimum of 15 of the 60 known osprey nests also were damaged by the fires. The loss of whitebark pine, Englemann spruce and tall stands of big sagebrush is of particular concern for certain avian species.

Despite pockets of devastation, satellite photos show the burned acreage to be a quarter million acres fewer than original estimates. Robinson believes that fire is a very benign force in such a vast area.

Robinson also believes the fires were therapeutic for the forest by killing diseased stands of lodgepole pine. Robinson said the fires not only destroyed hundreds of years of debris on the forest floor, fireproofing much of the park for generations to come, but also opened up new vistas for the public.

When tourists come to Yellowstone in the future, Robinson said they would be able to see more wildlife because the habitat has been improved and the viewing areas have been cleaned out.

"Natural processes constantly change," said Robinson, "but most change is imperceptible to those of us who live on this planet." People tend to become disturbed when their environment undergoes a violent change like it did that summer in Yellowstone, but Robinson said we need to adopt a less human outlook and start thinking in terms of "biological time."

That's easier said than done. People who are used to seeing wide expanses of green trees and grassy meadows are turned off by snags and soot after a forest fire.

"I am outraged," shouted Anna May Kline as she stood in front of her store in West Yellowstone and watched columns of smoke rise over the park.

"O-u-t-r-a-g-e-d..." screamed Kline. "Our national heritage is burning down. Even the Indians had respect for fire and to let it burn is a total outrage."

Many Native American Indian groups understood the critical role of fire in nature. Some Native American tribes even intentionally set fires on the Great Plains to help kill flies and mosquitoes, or to aid in attracting buffalo herds and other wildlife into areas of newly sprouted grasses that resulted following fires. Many early settlers also followed these practices.

Kline said people at park headquarters should have seen red flags flying as summer 1988 began, flags signalling the drought of the century. Kline said she and other concerned citizens wrote to Superintendent Robert Barbee warning him of the possibility of fire. Kline thinks Barbee should be hanged, "but I know he won't."

"We are going to have to re-think our policy, no question about it," said Barbee. "But the entire area here is not on fire because of some misguided policy." Barbee told townspeople in West Yellowstone that the fire threatening their town was man-made, and was aggressively fought from the beginning.

After the firestorm at Old Faithful, North Fork Incident Commander Denny Bungarz said, "It's going to take a lot more than people and equipment to solve

our problem. It's going to take a change in the weather."

Area commander Rick Gale, who was charged with setting priorities and allocating critical resources on the North Fork Fire, agreed there was no way to stop the fire. "Once these winds get over 10 miles per hour, the fires spot, and the lines won't hold them," said Gale, who compared the spotting to skipping a rock across a pond.

Asked how aggressively his people attacked the North Fork Fire, Gale said they were in a "tactical-mode," or full-suppression posture, since the fire entered the park from the Targhee National Forest. "There's speculation as to what we might have done with this fire," said Gale, "but that's just pure speculation about what might have been, could have been or should have been."

During a visit to a fire camp in late August, National Park Service Director William Penn Mott, Jr. defended the "natural-fire" policy. "I don't think you can blame anybody for what's happened," said Mott.

"This hysteria about fire policy being responsible for the whole park burning up is ridiculous," said Superintendent

Barbee at the time. "We are using high-tech firefighting methods, but the best we've been able to throw at the fires has not been enough to overcome them."

As Ron Platt, who owns three electronic instrument businesses in West Yellowstone, left a meeting with Barbee, he said if a popularity survey were taken around town, Barbee would come in last.

Across the street at the Western Inn, a marquee sign boldly proclaimed, "Welcome to West Yellowstone Barbee que."

"I think the Park Service blew it," said Cindy Murchison, who owns a condo in West Yellowstone.

When asked if he thinks the National Park Service blew it, Trevor Povah, who owns Deep Well Ranch about six miles out of town and Hamilton Stores, Inc., one of the major concessionaires in Yellowstone National Park, said, "Yeah! Everybody's working their buns off to get things back, but there's no way they can recoup. The park's gonna be a black forest for a hundred years."

Povah, a close personal friend of Interior Secretary Donald Hodel, said he thinks the fire could have been put out when it first crossed the park boundary, and he told Hodel the park personnel

A bull elk gathering his harem along a burned area near the Madison River.

35

As the fires blazed, so did the tempers of area residents who depended upon the tourist trade, which dropped dramatically until the fires were controlled.

It took more than forest fires to keep these fly fishermen from getting a line wet in the Firehole River near Old Faithful.

MICHAEL CRUMMETT

blew it. "But it's gone too far now. The goddamned park's gonna burn up."

"I've seen no information that we blew it," said Agriculture Secretary Richard Lyng, who accompanied Hodel to Yellowstone after the firestorm at Old Faithful.

"This is one of those once-in-50-years, once-in-100-years deals," said Lyng as he addressed a town meeting in West Yellowstone. "It's nice to lash out at people who are not doing a good job," but Lyng said he felt park personnel and the 25,000 civilian and military people who fought the fires did a good job last summer.

Hodel, Lyng and Assistant Secretary of Defense William Taft IV were sent to Yellowstone by President Reagan to see if

there was anything more that could be done to bring the fires under control.

"In spite of the best efforts we were able to put on this fire," said Hodel, "we were unable to bring it under control." But Secretary Hodel reminded his critics in the audience that the North Fork Fire was fought aggressively from the beginning.

Hodel's remarks were interrupted by laughter. Sensing disapproval, Hodel said he hasn't met anyone, though, who would suggest, "If we had the year to do over, we wouldn't do it differently."

Agriculture Secretary Lyng said, "This is not the time for recriminations." Lyng said he thought it was time to give the people charged with trying to put the

fires out all the support and encouragement they need. Hodel agreed that "Monday morning quarterbacking is tough on the people who are fighting the fires."

Wyoming Governor Mike Sullivan, who hosted the cabinet-level tour of Yellowstone, drew the loudest round of applause when he told the crowd that now is not the time to point fingers or debate policies. "Now is the time to put out fires," said Sullivan. "We can kick butts later."

From a purely economic viewpoint, the fires at Yellowstone couldn't have come at a worse time. They broke out when the tourist business was booming in early summer. Two major businesses in the park, TW Recreational Services, Inc. and Hamilton Stores, Inc. say the fires cost them millions.

"We lost $4.5 million in gross sales," said Steve Tedder, vice president and general manager at TW. "July, August and September are the months when most of the money is dropped in the park." The average tourist spends about $50 a day. "More from folks who stay at our hotels," said Tedder, who pointed to a survey in 1987 that shows each visitor had an average expenditure of $88 for lodging, $43 for travel, $54 for food and $40 for other items. But fires forced park officials to close entrances to the park and roads inside the park in late July, and that cut deeply into tourist revenues.

Tourist traffic dropped more than seven percent in July and almost 30 percent in August. When the North Fork Fire

threatened to destroy Old Faithful Inn in early September, TW Services shut down operations altogether, one month early. "Disastrous," said Tedder, "for 1,000 employees we had to lay off."

TW and Hamilton Stores operate snack bars, gift shops and lodges inside the park. When all nine of its locations are in operation, TW Services employs 2,200 people. Hamilton Stores has about 800 employees on the payroll, but on September 8, the day after the firestorm at Old Faithful, Hamilton had only one store open, and the only people shopping were reporters and an occasional firefighter.

In the first week of September, Tedder said only 25 percent of its 2,000 rooms were occupied at Old Faithful Inn and two other lodges, Lake Lodge and Mammoth Hot Springs Hotel.

The fires also hurt tourism in communities at the entrances to Yellowstone National Park. "This has been a total disaster," said Milt Toratti, a retired Army colonel who manages Lionshead Resort just outside Yellowstone's west entrance. Toratti said only 15 of 150 RV spaces were filled in September when the fires reached their peak. The year before, 93 of the spaces had been filled. Only 11 rooms at the Lionshead Resort Motel were filled in September 1988, compared to a full house a year before.

Much of the tourist business in the fall of the year is senior-oriented. Senior citizens traditionally wait until September, when parents put their kids in school, to visit Yellowstone. But in 1988

Swans cruise down the Madison River near West Yellowstone as fire continues to burn in the timber along the river bank.

Looking east down Main Street in West Yellowstone, tourists could see huge billows of smoke boiling skyward over the park.

Facing page: *A 100-foot-tall pine tree explodes in flames near Canyon Village. The rush of flames upward sends burning embers flying for as much as a half mile.*

hundreds of senior tours cancelled at the last moment cancelled when tour directors saw the streets of towns like West Yellowstone obliterated by smoke. Seniors are more susceptible than others to respiratory problems, and smoke only exacerbates any problem they might have.

People who did brave the smoke and came to West Yellowstone were what Toratti called "couple-hour people." They stayed for two hours, became discouraged when they learned the park was closed, and drove off.

Ken Takata, president of the Chamber of Commerce in West Yellowstone, said businesses, especially retail shops, experienced losses of 30 to 40 percent over the summer. But most businesses were able to recoup some of their losses through sales to civilian and military firefighters and curiosity-seekers.

Milt Toratti said his restaurant was able to provide catering services to the government during the "Siege of Yellowstone," but Toratti says he couldn't recover the kind of revenue tourists spend, because of ceilings on the prices of meals and the fact that no gratuities are charged.

The fires also heavily impacted outfitters in Montana who had to cancel hunting trips when Governor Ted Schwinden cancelled the first couple weeks of the hunting season.

"The fire crucified my business," said outfitter Merritt Pride of West Yellowstone. Although he lost trips that had been booked a year in advance, Pride agreed with the governor's ban on outdoor recreation at the height of the fires. "It wasn't a question of whether another fire would be started by man," said Pride, "it was just when and where."

Although an interagency review of the Yellowstone fires, the North Fork Fire in particular, appears to absolve Park Superintendent Barbee of any blame for what happened, Merritt Pride believes Barbee missed two golden opportunities to gain the upper hand on the North Fork Fire.

"Once when it crossed into the park from the Targhee [National Forest] and it involved less than 100 acres," said Pride, "and secondly on August 12 when we got a little rain." The fire lay down, didn't move, but Pride claims park crews didn't seize the initiative and go in and mop up the ground fire. Once the winds picked up, Pride said, "It was too late."

WILLIAM R. SALLAZ

MICHAEL H. FRANCIS

During the height of the fires, you could drive for miles in Yellowstone without seeing another vehicle on the road.

Clouds of smoke from the Hellroaring Fire look like an atomic bomb has been dropped on the park near the North Entrance Arch at Gardiner, Montana.

Steve Tedder of TW Services looked to the future. "The falls, canyons, rivers and wildlife are still here," said Tedder, "and by the time kids who come to the park in the near future return again, the trees will be taller than they will be."

Up until 1987, more kids and their parents came to Yellowstone from California than from any other state, but Californians now are having to take a back seat to their international cousins who account for 20 percent of Yellowstone's tourist business—people from Canada, the United Kingdom, West Germany and the Orient. Some of them witnessed the fires of 1988.

Melko Giebing and five friends from Holland were amazed at the size of the flames. "They were so big," said Giebing, who took pictures at the Old Faithful complex the day it burned. It startled Giebing to see the flames travel so fast and throw off showers of embers.

"They were so unpredictable," said Giebing, who still had difficulty breathing after inhaling so much ash and smoke. "It was very hot, we were very close," recalled Giebing as he and his friends loaded their luggage into a rental car and prepared to head to the airport for a flight home.

Kirsten DeYoung of Amsterdam, the Netherlands, and her American host, Susan Hoerger from Palo Alto, were wearing tee-shirts they had bought in West Yellowstone. Emblazoned on the front were the words, "I Survived The Fires At Yellowstone." Thousands of tee-shirts were sold in West Yellowstone and other communities around the park.

DeYoung said she couldn't wait to get home and tell her friends about "the BIG FIRE in the West."

Zoey Lewis, a tourist from Denver who drove to Yellowstone after smelling smoke in Colorado for weeks, said, "It's heartbreaking, but it's interesting, because history is being made right now."

Mild weather and curiosity about the damage from 1988's summer fires helped Yellowstone National Park set an attendance record in October 1988. Attendance then increased by almost 50,000 people, or more than 39 percent, compared to the same month the year before. Park officials counted 175,019 people visiting the park in October 1988, compared to a total of 125,597, which had been the previous record for October. In the previous 10 years, an average of 100,500 people visited the park in the tenth month of the year.

The October figures brought the number of people to visit the park during its summer season, May 1 to October 1, 1988, to almost 2.07 million, a 16 percent decline from 1987, but Superintendent Barbee said the 1988 summer attendance represented only a 5 percent decline from the 10-year average of almost 2.17 million. The summer attendance record, 2.47 million, was set in 1978.

"But what about two, three, five, ten years down the road?" asked Interior Secretary Hodel as he wound up a whirlwind tour of fire-ravaged areas around Old Faithful last September. "That is the real follow-on test," said Hodel, who spoke about the federal government's commitment to the rebirth of Yellowstone. "The natural features are still here, wildlife, et cetera, and we need to develop programs that will encourage people to visit Yellowstone."

"If we don't," said Hayes Kirby, who operates the Anvil Inn and the Grizzly Lodge in Silver Gate, "these gateway communities to Yellowstone National Park will become ghost towns."

Normally there would not be any attempt to plant new trees after a fire in a national forest, but Interior Secretary Donald Hodel said it was clear from what he saw in Yellowstone last summer that vegetation would have to be replenished in order to restore the beauty of the U.S.'s first national park.

The Chairman of the Post-Fire Ecological Assessment Committee disagrees. Duke University botanist Norman L. Christensen recommended that park officials not reseed burned meadows or plant new trees in burned forests. "Nature has all the regenerative potential it needs for these ecosystems, without human interference," Christensen said.

While man debated reseeding, Mother Nature began the healing process. Even while some of the fires smoldered, a blanket of soothing snow spread over the open wounds.

While man debated reseeding Yellowstone in late summer 1988, Mother Nature began the healing process. Even while some of the fires smoldered, a blanket of soothing snow spread over the open wounds.

CHAPTER FIVE

Death of an old friend

MICHAEL H. FRANCIS

"Don't be disturbed by the devastation you saw. It's not as devastating as it appeared on the surface."

That's how George Robinson, Chief Naturalist at Yellowstone National Park, viewed the fires that swept the park in the summer of 1988.

Six years before, when Robinson accepted his current assignment and came to Yellowstone, he chose a word to inject into every interpretative project he touched. RENAISSANCE became "the buzz word," but little did George Robinson know at the time he chose that word that it would describe what is now occurring in the nation's premier park.

As 60-mile-per-hour winds howled through the cavernous International Fly Fishing Center in West Yellowstone—which became the nerve center of information during those dark, discouraging days in early September1988—a meek man in a green National Park Service uniform was quietly moving about the room, relieving the minds of those who silently mourned the death of a great forest.

"Obviously a lot of the trees have been destroyed," said district naturalist Joe Halliday, "but that doesn't mean total devastation."

"What we're seeing is the old forest going, but we know a new one will return. As soon as it rains or snows, there'll be a lot of green grass sprouting in the ash.

"It's like the death of an old friend. We can't believe he's gone. There is a period of mourning, but the hurt doesn't last forever."

"Yellowstone was a ticking time bomb," said Patrick Pontes, a veteran firefighter from Los Padres National Forest in California. All that was needed was someone to light the fuse.

"This was a fire of historic proportions. We had old brush, old timber: 150- to 200-year-old trees," said Pontes as he watched clouds of smoke rise east of Madison Campground like the mushroom clouds of nuclear war. "And that's historic when they start burning."

In a normal year, two or three good rain showers would soak Yellowstone National Park and wet down the underbrush, but not in 1988. The lack of rainfall that spring, combined with one of the country's worst droughts in 50 years, super-dried the forest. Despite the drought, Halliday said park officials believed fires would not be a large problem in their part of the country as they sought to achieve a diversified forest. After all, the largest natural fire in the park's history burned

RICK GRAETZ

Fires hopscotched across Yellowstone in 1988. There is a mosaic effect to the burn west of Tower Junction.

Facing page: Forests do recover from fires. Here an outfitter leads a pack train through regrowth of the Beaver-Heart Fire, which burned in 1979. Although lodgepole pine will take years to return, sagebrush already covers the ground.

only about 18,000 acres at Heart Lake in 1931. Officials apparently counted on the climate and weather conditions like those of the past to provide the moisture they needed to reduce the danger of fire.

"But the very dry conditions we had, added an entirely new element that has not been in the textbook, past records or computer fire models," said Halliday

I remember bumping into Denny Bungarz one night in a fire camp. It was early September. And there was no end in sight to the fires that had plagued the park for the past three months. Asked how long they might burn, Bungarz, the Incident Commander on the North Fork Fire, just shook his head. "It's like a baseball game," said Bungarz. "Mother Nature has thrown us a lot of curves."

Asked where in the game we were, Bungarz smiled and said, "Somewhere in the latter innings, and I'm praying we don't go into extra innings."

Ecologists have known for many years that wildfire is essential to the evolution of a natural setting. When fires are suppressed, normal plant succession is stagnated, and biological diversity is reduced or altered.

Research into Yellowstone's prehistory has shown that on the park's northern range, in places like Lamar Valley, fires occurred one to four times a century, while over the vast extent of the park's subalpine forests, the fire interval was more typically 200 to 400 years. In other words, Yellowstone was long overdue for a major fire. Joe Halliday agrees with Chief Naturalist George Robinson, who believed the fires were therapeutic for the aging forest. For example, some plants, such as lodgepole pine, need fire to renew themselves. Immediately after a fire, seeds are released from heat-sensitive cones.

When park plant ecologist Don Despain documented seed densities in some of the forests burned in 1988, he found densities ranging from 50,000 to 1 million seeds per acre. Some of these will survive the appetites of mice, squirrels and birds and eventually produce a forest much like the one that burned on the site.

Despain figured that within five years, there might be 1,000 seedlings per acre, depending upon how much competition they face from grasses, wildflowers and shrubs.

Lodgepole pine will slowly return over a 10-year period. The experts say 40 years after the fire, most of the burned areas will be young forests again.

This kind of "ecological revolution" comes around only once every 200 or 300 years, and that explains why Joe Halliday and other scientists were so happy about the changing of the guard in Yellowstone.

With the floor of the forest now open to light for the first time in several hundred years, an abundance of wildflowers, grasses and wild strawberries will provide ample food for small rodents, other mammals and birds that was not available in the old forest. In addition to stimulating new plant forms, the fire opened new vistas for research and study, for example, on birds and mammals as they return to the burned areas.

Biologists now will have an opportunity to study tree growth from the ground up, and also the effects of fire on soils, watersheds and animal behavior.

"And although we tend to grieve for the old friend who has died," said Joe Halliday, "those of us in biological circles look forward to a new friend who's coming on scene."

Strike and move

MICHAEL H. FRANCIS

More than 1,000 miles of fire line was dug into the ridges and mountains in Yellowstone National Park during the 1988 fires. It was hot, dangerous work.

"Strike and move," shouted Cal Peño, a strike team leader from Laguna, New Mexico as his Native-American crew scrambled up a steep bank near Antelope Creek and attacked a forest fire that was turning lodgepole pine and Douglas fir into flaming torches.

"Strike and move" is a tactic some fire teams use to dig a fire line quickly. The 20-man team lines up one behind the other, with about 18 inches between each two men. They crouch over and dig their pulaskis into the earth. (See facing page, bottom photo.)

As the name "strike and move" implies, the first man in line strikes the ground with a pulaski and flips over a large chunk of sod before moving farther up the slope. The man following in his footsteps never looks up; he just takes a swipe at untouched ground. By the time the last man takes a swing at the ground, there's a freshly-gouged fireline about 30 yards up the hill.

It's amazing how fast a well trained fire team like the one from Laguna could move in burning timber.

"Watch out for snags, guys!" shouted Peño, who is responsible for his crew's safety. Peño's crew started out with 20 men, but injuries cut the crew almost by half. "We're tired," said Peño, "but our spirits are still high, and the team is still pulling together."

Down the road it was a different story—a story of frustration—as Joe Leonard Gomez and Ricardo Lucero from Taos, New Mexico lay back on a bank and watched the timber burn above them.

Gomez's crew had been begging all afternoon for another 450-foot section of hose so they could reach the fire. But none came. So the men stretched out and watched as a comrade sprayed the grass in front of them. "What the hell can we do?" asked Gomez. "That line doesn't reach over there."

Lucero, who was dead-tired after 21 days of running up one hill and down another stamping out fires, said he's been on bigger fires than the one at Antelope Creek, but none so frustrating.

"Yeah," said Gomez, "the crew is tired of all this B.S. of jumping back and forth from one hot spot to another."

"This fire is too big for ground teams," said Lucero. "What we need are slurry bombers, but the Park Service

There was a lot of frustration, but most was the result of men running until they almost dropped.

Left: *Marines from the 1st Battalion, 5th Marine Division wasted no time setting up camp at Madison, where they bivouacked.*
Below: *A GI getting down to basics with his pulaski, the two-edged basic weapon of a firefighter.*

Facing page: *A U.S. Marine from Camp Pendleton, California engaged in hand-to-hand combat with Mother Nature. More than 4,500 men and women proved to be a valuable asset in fighting the 1988 fires in Yellowstone.*

doesn't want to stain the landscape with the retardant."

A pumper truck from Georgetown, California finally came down the mountain road with its siren blaring as if the crew were going to a house fire. A few minutes after charging the line, the water was gone. "We only carry 800 gallons," said Chief Jack Anderson. No one apparently thought about re-supply from tanker trucks like the ones that haul as much as 4,000 gallons of water to swimming pools.

There was a lot of frustration at the fires, most of it the result of men running until they almost dropped. Some crews worked 12 hours a day, seven days a week, 14 days on, two off, 14 on before being relieved.

Army Staff Sgt. Darryl Williams of Jacksonville, Florida summed up the frustration: "We would battle a fire all day long, only to see another fire someplace else and we'd say we're losing the war."

A backfire that backfired

STEVE DOWELL; BOZEMAN DAILY CHRONICLE

What I'm looking at right now, I wouldn't believe," said Dr. William Hruza, Jr. as he got out of his Ford Bronco in front of the summer home he owns in Silver Gate, Montana. As his wife, Marge, swept her eyes along the fire-scarred ridges above Soda Butte Creek, which runs through town, she sobbed, "Poor forest."

Hruza's daughter Chris, a flight attendant for Northwest Airlines in Minneapolis, also cried. "It just makes me sick. No excuse for this. Absolutely no excuse," she said.

"This area will never look the same; never in my lifetime," said Hruza. "It's a sad point in my life. I'm 71 and I wish I had never seen this."

Hruza was a Navy surgeon who stormed ashore with the Marines on Iwo Jima. The scorched earth with its ankle-deep, black ash in the surrounding mountains reminded him of the volcanic ash on that island in the Northern Pacific where he won the Silver Star in World War II. After the first day of combat, Hruza was the only doctor left alive in his battalion.

"Before we were forced to evacuate our home here in Silver Gate on Sunday, September 4," said Hruza, "this area looked like a war zone with columns of soldiers marching down Main Street and bombers dropping retardant on the fires which raged out of control above town on the ridgeline."

Ironically, the fire that swept through the Soda Butte drainage the day after Labor Day was not a runaway forest fire. The wall of flames that roared past Silver Gate and burned to within 50 feet of Cooke City, three miles down the road, was part of a "backburn" designed to keep the Storm Creek Fire from burning into the Soda Butte drainage. Backfires are probably the most common forest fire tactic, but backfires can backfire.

Hayes Kirby, owner of the Grizzly Lodge in Silver Gate, lives a quarter of a mile from where the backburn was set. "Three hours later, the fire ran over us," said Kirby.

The fire line we visited was a wide swath of timber cut down with chain saws and allowed to fall into the center of the cut. No attempt had been made to police the area and fireproof the line.

Confronted about the backburn that backfired, a high-ranking official said, "It was just one of those things when you've got to make your best decision." If a backfire isn't lit in time, and the fire comes, you won't have a chance to light one, and you run the risk of being overrun.

Firefighters retreating from the backfire they have just set.

Facing page: *It's frightening to look up and see a wall of flame in your face, but this scene was repeated many times in Yellowstone National Park in 1988.*

Based on forecasts by weather service personnel and fire behavior specialists that the approaching fire would get into the Pebble Creek drainage and roar into the narrow canyon like a blowtorch, it was decided that the only way to stop that from happening was to have an area of "burned-up fuel" between the Storm Creek Fire and the gateway communities of Silver Gate and Cooke City.

With the same information again, fire officials would have lit the same backfires. They expected 50-mile-per-hour winds behind the fire, which would have taken every house in the valley. They argue that the backfires didn't burn up that much acreage around Silver Gate and Cooke City, but spotting from them did.

"The backfire was a tactical move," conceded Ralph Glidden, owner of the historic Cooke City Store, "but as it turned out, only the backfire burned us." As far as Glidden and other townspeople are concerned, officials "pushed the panic button."

"Totally incompetent," said Dave Majors of Silver Gate, who ignored threats from the sheriff to lock up those who didn't obey his evacuation order.

"The backfires were set long before there was a threat to the towns," said Majors, who is aggravated that fire lines like the one atop Pebble Creek Pass were abandoned before they were finished.

The backfires, and the spotting that occurred when the winds increased, melted the plastic pipe leading to Silver Gate's water supply. But when Majors put in 1,000 feet of new line and got the water flowing again, it wasn't a half hour until a U.S. Forest Service representative knocked on his door.

"He wanted to know if there was any old burned pipe lying in the middle of the burned forest," said Majors, "'cause he deemed that would be unsightly, and the official reminded me that our permit would not allow such an unsightly mess left in the forest."

The visit really frosted Dave Majors. "I told the man it was about time he cut us some slack, and it would be advisable if he got off my property immediately."

Folks in Silver Gate and Cooke City are an independent lot. They don't ask for favors. Most of them just want to be left alone. Take Tommy Garrison, whose 16-by-24-foot cabin up Lulu Creek Trail was

47

Above: *A lone firefighter back-burning in a stand of lodgepole pine near Storm Creek in Montana. Fire officials hoped to deny approaching fire its fuel by such controlled burns. But this one backfired when high winds set the forest on fire.*

Right: *Bulldozers at work clearing a fireline. The fires at Yellowstone in 1988 were so fierce that they often jumped even the widest fireline.*

destroyed by the backburn. I found him sleeping in his 1980 MG convertible next to the Cooke City Store.

"Warmest place I've found," snorted Tommy, who has lived alone in the woods outside of town for 30 years.

Garrison, who is 84, has a reputation for being cantankerous, even for shooting first and asking questions later when strangers approach. He almost died the winter after the fires, as the result of sleeping in the front seat of his MG in an aluminum space blanket for several weeks.

"If I had been able to get up there [authorities wouldn't let him through a road-block] I could have saved my stuff," said Garrison as he wiped his running nose with a handkerchief, one of the few things he had left, "but they tell me the fire went through the woods so quickly, it would have taken everything in front of it, including humans."

The heat was tremendous. It cracked boulders and melted huge steel spikes Garrison had used to nail logs together in his cabin.

A lot of people in Cooke City were concerned for Garrison when his cabin burned down. Bob Smith, owner of Bearclaw Cabins, offered to give Garrison a sleeping bag when he learned Garrison was sleeping behind the wheel of his sports car. But Garrison refused the offers, saying he didn't want to start accumulating things until he had a place to keep them.

As of this writing, Garrison lived in a room at the All Seasons on the east side of town. Motel owner Darrell Crabb said Garrison was welcome to stay there for the rest of his life, or until he decided to move on.

Tommy Garrison never has accepted acts of kindness the way most people do. For example, Hayes Kirby remembered the day his girlfriend baked Garrison some chocolate chip cookies, and left them on the doorstep of his cabin.

The next morning, when Kirby opened the door at the Grizzly Lodge, there were the cookies, with a note that read simply, "No thanks. Cookies attract bears."

A grizzly bear once ate the canvas top off Tommy's yellow MG, and until he could afford to buy a new top, he drove the convertible without one for several winters.

Asked how many miles he had on his car, Garrison smiled a toothless grin and said proudly, "47,500...but that's not accurate." Apparently the stem to the odometer cable broke off years ago, and he never bothered having it fixed.

Garrison's cabin was one of four lost

Tommy Garrison lived alone in the woods outside of Cook City for 30 years—until the backfire destroyed his cabin.

Tommy Garrison beside his MG convertible, his temporary and freezing home after his cabin burned.

when the backburn backfired, but he didn't bother to sue the government. Others did. In the months following the fire, U.S. Forest Service officials began processing more than two dozen claims. Residents and businesses filed more than $1 million in damage claims against the government, whose attorneys had to determine whether negligence or nature caused the damage.

Sixteen of the damage claims, totaling $525,000, stemmed from the Storm Creek Fire that destroyed Tommy Garrison's cabin. Among the claims were requests for restitution for damage to cabins and fences, a motel, an outfitting camp and a water system that Dave Majors replaced.

Similar claims totaling $563,000, from fires in the Shoshone National Forest, also were being reviewed. Those stemmed primarily from the loss of mobile homes in a subdivision northwest of Cody, Wyoming. One outfitter claimed $18,000 in losses of income and supplies.

Yellowstone National Park spokesperson Joan Anzelmo says there were several small claims for personal property loss within the park, including claims from firefighters who lost items such as watches and glasses. However, decisions on the claims could take months or years.

In the meantime, Tommy Garrison said he would make do with what he has.

Editor's note: Tommy Garrison died at his home, the All Seasons Motel, of natural causes in the spring of 1989.

Presidential fact-finding mission

GUY R. HIGBEE

After the firestorm at Old Faithful on September 7, President Reagan dispatched a fact-finding team to Yellowstone National Park to assess the damage and determine what needed to be done to put the fires out and what steps should be taken to prevent similar fires in the future.

Interior Secretary Donald Hodel, who oversees the National Park Service, and Agriculture Secretary Richard Lyng, who is responsible for the U.S. Forest Service, took a brief but enlightening bus tour through a 30-mile stretch of the park.

Both Hodel and Lyng expressed surprise at what they saw on the way to Old Faithful. "I think it's devastating," said Hodel as he viewed scorched stands of lodgepole pine along the Madison River. "It's a disaster and I think we've only seen a part of it."

"You have to be sad at what you see," said Lyng as he boarded the bus to continue the trip to Old Faithful. "Just look at it—DEVASTATING."

This was Lyng's first trip to Yellowstone since the fires broke out in June. Hodel had toured the park in mid-July, pronouncing the natural-burn policy a good one; by summer's end, Hodel was singing a different tune. Asked whether the fire-fighting policies would change, Hodel said, "I think they'd have to." Even President Reagan, who said he didn't know there was such a policy, believed it should be amended.

It started raining as the presidential fact-finding mission, which included Assistant Secretary of Defense William Taft IV, approached Lower Geyser Basin. By the time the chartered bus pulled up in front of historic Old Faithful Inn, the rain was really coming down—a fact that did not go unnoticed by Donald Hodel.

"Those of you who were with Secretary Lyng on the drought task force know that when he went on that trip, it rained either during or immediately after every stop," said Hodel. But Lyng quickly pointed out one problem of bringing rain to a place like Yellowstone. "People will say for crying out loud, why didn't you come sooner," laughed Lyng.

As if on cue, the famous geyser at Old Faithful shot a stream of steam skyward as the two cabinet members stood near the observation ring.

At one point in the whirlwind tour of the battleground at Old Faithful, Hodel talked to a park ranger who a couple of days earlier had hosed down some of the buildings so they wouldn't catch fire from burning embers that rained down.

The ranger said he hoped Hodel would make an "educated and wise decision" as to what happened at Yellowstone, but before the ranger could respond to a reporter's question about what he thought that decision should be, he was interrupted by Hodel's press secretary who said, "Sorry about that, but we've got to move along."

Before flying to Boise, Idaho to be briefed at the Interagency Fire Control Center on fires that were ravaging seven other western states, Hodel and Lyng held a news conference at the International Fly Fishing Center in West Yellowstone.

"I didn't think I would see anything like Mount St. Helens," said Lyng, "but I did here." Hodel hastened to say that the natural features of Yellowstone National Park were not touched. "They're still here," said Hodel, "and so are the major facilities." But Hodel admitted personnel did not fight the North Fork Fire, which burned almost a half million acres, as aggressively as they should have.

Hodel and Lyng promised a thorough investigation and gave a task force until December 15, 1988 to report its findings to them.

The 10-member Fire Management Policy Review Team, composed of professionals from the departments of Interior and Agriculture, analyzed the summer's severe fire season, identified shortcomings in fire-management policy, and suggested improvements in federal fire-management plans.

The 25-page report said that while the basic objectives of federal fire management policies, including "prescriptions" that set forth how some lightning-caused fires should be allowed to burn under defined conditions, are sound, "The policies themselves need to be refined, strengthened, and reaffirmed."

In addition to strengthening the fire policy, the team recommended that: regional and national contingency plans be developed to contain prescribed fires under extreme conditions; agencies consider planned ignitions to complement prescribed natural fire programs and to reduce hazard fuels; and additional research and analysis on weather, fire behavior, fire history and integration of fire information be carried out so that future fire-management programs can be more effective in reducing the risk of wildfires.

The report stated that, "Dissemination of information before and during prescribed natural fires needs to be improved. There needs to be greater public participation in the development of fire management plans."

In many cases, the team found fire-management plans for individual parks or wilderness areas in national forests "do not meet current policies, and the prescriptions in them are inadequate."

During the investigation, the team of experts heard claims that some managers, with philosophies advocating "naturalness" above all else, intentionally allowed fires to burn outside of prescriptions and did not take the appropriate actions to suppress wildfires. However, evidence in draft reviews of the major fires at Yellowstone did not support allegations that these fires were allowed to burn freely as long as they were not expected to leave the boundary of a park or wilderness. The team did not have a mandate to investigate, verify or disprove the allegations.

In an exclusive interview shortly after his retirement, former Secretary of the Interior Donald Hodel offered this writer his feelings about the summer of 1988.

"Now that I've had several months to think about the fires, we really weren't able to do much except protect structures such as the Old Faithful Inn and protect gateway communities such as West Yellowstone, Silver Gate and Cooke City.

"It's like the guy who takes an 800-pound gorilla for a walk. Question: 'Where do you walk him?' Answer: 'Anywhere he wants to go.' That's how the fire was. Once it got started, it went anywhere it wanted to go."

Hodel saw his role in the fire scenario as that of cheerleader. At the time he visited in September, morale was sagging. Hodel believes Park Service personnel and others were totally unequipped to deal with a firestorm of criticism in the media.

He said, "If we had perfect foresight in early July we would have put 9,000 troops on the fireline, but by September the fires were simply too large."

About reaction to the "natural-fire" policy, Hodel added:

"We didn't hear much, if anything, from our friends in the environmental community. They didn't give us any support until the heat was off."

His interpretation was that "leaders of environmental groups in this country are so highly partisan, it's almost impossible for them to say anything good about a Republican administration.

"They let us swing in the wind until I said we can't let this happen again."

Looking to the future, Hodel said, "It's clear that we have to reduce fuel buildups around facilities such as Old Faithful Inn, Grant Village, Mammoth and other recreational areas—but we have to let the old

The powerful fires were like the joke about taking an 800-pound gorilla for a walk. Where? Anywhere he wants to go.

Facing page: *Then-Secretary of the Interior Donald Hodel holding a news conference at Old Faithful three days after a firestorm raged across the southern side of the complex. In retrospect, Hodel said there was no way to stop the fires at Yellowstone.*

forest burn. There has to be prescribed burning, and it may be necessary in extremely dry conditions to jump on fires sooner.

"I know that people downwind are going to simply go bananas with the smoke, but we have to reduce some of the fuel in the park."

Commenting on the controversy over use of bulldozers to dig firelines, Hodel stated, "It can take a thousand years for Mother Nature to heal the scars left by bulldozed firelines. However, Mother Nature can reforest an area in less than a hundred years.

"When you're in a commercial forest, you've got no choice—you use bulldozers. But in a national park, you've got to weigh the consequence of scarring the ground.

"If Superintendent Barbee had used bulldozers at the outset of the North Fork Fire we would have heard screams of outrage from the park's constituency."

Summarizing this major event of his last summer as Secretary of the Interior, Hodel said that "in many ways, Yellowstone was like a battlefield. The fires were moving so rapidly, and as in combat situations, communications were always a problem."

The Chairman of the House Agriculture Committee planned hearings on how the U.S. Forest Service handled the stubborn 1988 blazes that scorched the West, including almost half of Yellowstone National Park.

"The major problem is that in speaking to people from the area, you speak to two and you get three opinions," said Rep. Kika De La Garza, a Texas Democrat. "The best thing to do is sit down and have them all put it on the record, and then sift through what happened, and see if anything needs to be done," said the chairman.

De La Garza planned to focus the hearings on forest fire practices and the question, "Can a catastrophe of that nature be avoided or was it a catastrophe?"

Two Senate subcommittees, one on Public Lands, National Parks and Forests and the other on Conservation and Forestry, held joint hearings on September 29, 1988.

The issue of fire suppression policy became a political hot potato, but Senator James McClure, R-Idaho, said he hoped the devastation of 1988 would open the public's eyes to the need for better management of our public forests.

But in some ways, McClure said, Congress is just as much to blame for what happened as anyone else. Senator John Melcher, D-Montana, agreed. "We knew a natural burn policy was being followed, and we the Congress permitted it," said Melcher. Melcher believed some of the inclination toward a natural burn policy was to save money by not hiring as many firefighters and by letting some forests rid themselves of dead trees.

"The natural-fire policy worked for the past 16 years since it was implemented in 1972," said McClure. "But this year [1988] it didn't."

But before anyone got the idea he was throwing stones, McClure said Congress should examine its own glass house first.

Unlike officials at Yellowstone National Park who believe 1988's summer fires have fireproofed the park for centuries to come, Senator McClure believes what happened will almost certainly happen again.

"We've been warned by land managers for years," testified McClure, "that long-term suppression of fires was going to lead to devastation."

According to Norman Christensen, a Duke University forestry professor who advises the National Park Service on fire management, "Yellowstone was like a volcano ready to explode."

"Without question, those fires constituted a major natural disaster," said George S. Dunlop, Assistant Secretary, Special Services, U.S. Department of Agriculture.

Wilderness areas and Yellowstone National Park in particular are managed under an objective that allows natural processes to operate with a minimum of human intervention or management. Harvesting timber is prohibited, and consequently these areas contain millions of acres of mature (and often dead and dying) lodgepole pine.

George Dunlop said a primary factor that made it so difficult to suppress the Greater Yellowstone Area fires was that huge areas of tinder-dry forestland had no road access. "There is little that humans can do to suppress fires in such situations," said Dunlop, "when fuel moisture drops as low as it was and fires are fanned by hot, dry winds."

With respect to the Yellowstone fires, Dunlop said the decision to allow some natural fires to burn as prescribed fires seemed reasonable early in the summer. "In retrospect, however, aggressive action should have been taken on all fires in the area," said Dunlop, "although it's questionable whether suppression would have been successful."

Other witnesses at the Senate hearing testified that budget cuts and errors in applying the "natural-fire" policy may have fanned the flames.

PATRICK CONE

Interior Secretary Donald Hodel said the Interior Department may have erred in allowing a large volume of dead timber to accumulate near developments in the park.

"For nearly 100 years," testified Hodel, "it was the general policy to suppress wildfires whenever possible or practical, especially after devastating fires earlier in this century." But Hodel confessed this policy only contributed to a buildup of fuels in many parks and wilderness areas in the West.

In addition, budget cuts over the last seven or eight years had reduced the U.S. Forest Service corps of seasonal firefighters by 25 percent, said Dale Robertson, chief of the U.S. Forest Service.

But regardless of the mistakes seen in hindsight, the fires still may have been unquenchable, said Dunlop.

The Park Service said that the most unfortunate misconception about the firefighting efforts in Yellowstone National Park may have been that human beings can always control fire if they really want to; however, the raw, unbridled power of the fires cannot be overemphasized.

At a joint House subcommittee hearing on U.S. fire policy, Rep. Ron Marlenee, a Montana Republican, said, "In the private sector, it [fire] would be called arson. In the bureaucracy and among environmental groups, it's viewed as God's will."

Although, at the same hearing, Dunlop defended the use of fire, he said government agencies with a voice in forest management should establish better communication, use more planned fires to reduce fuel buildup, and prepare contingency plans for fire control under extreme conditions such as those in 1988.

Estimates of burned acreage are shocking at first glance; it is even more shocking to fly over an active fire and look down through the smoke and see lodgepole pines scattered like jackstraws. But Yellowstone did not look like the lunar landscape regularly portrayed in the media at the time.

Most of the fires hopscotched through the back country, laying waste to some sections of the forest, leaving others untouched.

The mammoth fires at Yellowstone burned more than timber and sagebrush. They seared the emotions of the American public as well. The park has received thousands of calls and letters from people expressing a range of emotions including anger, fear, sadness and grief.

Since many of the letters came from children, it was decided to build a Children's Fire Trail telling the story of the 1988 fires and how they would shape the park in the years to come. This trail is funded by contributions from children, their families and teachers all over the country, and the trail will be dedicated in their honor.

As envisioned, the $125,500 trail features interpretive exhibits and a boardwalk path about one mile long that will take people through a variety of forest types, including areas that were totally burned, partially burned, and untouched by the flames. An area that had been burned in the past allows visitors to see first-hand the long-term process of forest recovery.

Most of the fires hopscotched through the back country, laying waste to some sections of the forest, leaving others untouched.

An army of reporters gather at Old Faithful for a briefing by National Park Service personnel. Between July 21 and September 21, there were more than 3,000 media people in Yellowstone National Park covering the "ecological event" of the past 300 years.

On the line with the military

As Interior Secretary Donald Hodel, Agriculture Secretary Richard Lyng and Assistant Defense Secretary William Taft IV prepared to leave Yellowstone National Park after a brief visit with the troops and a tour of the battlefield, a brisk wind kicked up, and fires jumped lines along the entire northern front from Duck Creek, north of fire command headquarters in West Yellowstone, to Tower Junction.

The leading edge of the fire swept across a grassy steppe and roared into Gallatin Canyon.

"It's just a mess of flames on both sides of the road for four or five miles," said Gallatin County Sheriff Ron Cutting, whose deputies were manning a roadblock at the junction of Routes 287 and 191. To the east, a huge column of smoke was on the run north.

SHAKE AND BAKE

Two platoons of soldiers from 1st Battalion, 11th U.S. Field Artillery (the "1/11") were deployed just east of the community of Duck Creek.

"It sounded like a freight train coming through the timber," said Barry Hottel of Clear Lake, California. Hottel was the U.S. Forest Service "guru" assigned to the army unit from Fort Lewis, Washington. It was his responsibility to see that they didn't get in over their heads and get hurt. Hottel had his marching orders from Yellowstone fire commands and they were simple: "Protect life and property, but above all protect life. Firefighters will not be put in jeopardy."

Hottel, a veteran firefighter with 20 years of eating smoke under his belt, found himself cut off at one point when the fire broke out and started running toward the Gallatin National Forest.

"We had to jump back into the burn areas," said Hottel, "when the fire jumped a dozer line." Hottel and his army strike team stayed in the burn for almost an hour. Some of the troops with him got scared when the smoke blotted out the sun and the forest became deathly dark. Hottel tried to keep his team away from the approaching flames as he worked his way downwind and picked his way to safety.

"The trees were exploding in our faces," said Hottel as he watched the blaze head north. "It was like having the forest filled with gasoline."

"Once we hopped into the burn areas," said Eddie Fox of Maui, Hawaii, "a couple of the guys feared it was SHAKE AND BAKE TIME," a term used to describe the de-

ABOVE: MICHAEL H. FRANCIS; INSET: ROSS SIMPSON

WILLIAM R. SALLAZ

ployment of a fire shelter. The men with Fox began scraping the floor of the forest down to bare dirt and were ready to hop under their fire shelters and let the flames roll over them. "But Hottel got them moving and got us out of there on the double," said Fox.

The most frightening part of being in a forest fire is not knowing which way to run. "If it hadn't been for our team leaders," said Joe Harrison of Prattsville, Arkansas, "we would have lost some guys in there."

The 1/11 had been in Yellowstone for three weeks prior to the Battle of Duck Creek. They were brought along slowly, first hitting the Hunter Fire where they mopped up after strike teams. The artillerymen then moved into the Huck Fire, where they were used in hot-line constructions, but their real baptism by fire came at Duck Creek on September 10.

"The smoke was incredible, you could barely breathe," said Patrick Daughtery of Barnsville, Vermont. "My nose was running and my eyes were stinging but Barry kept his cool and led us out of there."

Similar sentiments were echoed by members of Daughtery's platoon, who survived their brush with death. "It really got dark," said John Massey of Kansas City, Missouri. "We couldn't see the sun." Massey said he had difficulty breathing and seeing although he had a bandana across his nose and mouth and goggles over his eyes.

Massey and the rest of the men did exactly what Hottel told them to do, and lived to laugh about their experience.

"Hope we don't have to do that again," said Mike Meneghetti of Dalton, Illinois.

The fires that jumped the lines and ran wild across the northern end of Yellowstone National Park on September 10 were driven by 20- to 40-mile-per-hour winds with gusts to 60 miles per hour.

Driving across the top of the park from West Yellowstone through Norris, Canyon Village and Tower Junction offered a stark panorama of Mother Nature's awesome power. The Petrified Forest just up the road from Roosevelt Lodge looked like Dak To in the Central Highlands of South Vietnam after fighter bombers scorched the trees black with napalm. Hundreds of huge trees lay splintered.

The only humans I saw that day were a couple of Bureau of Land Management employees near Mount Washburn. Marty Hunter and David Haney were forward observers, mapping the fire burning below us in the Antelope Valley and calculating its rate of spread.

Hunter and Haney were assigned to the Hellroaring Fire. Their boss wanted to know how fast the Wolf Lake Fire was spreading through the valley.

"It's impressive," said Haney, who had been watching the fire advance through some of the park's prime grizzly bear habitat for two days. "We watched the fires advance at the rate of one mile an hour at Mount Washburn. The flames leaped 300 feet into the air, and spotted six to eight miles in one day. That's a firestorm. Those of us who work out here in the West don't see that very often. It's awesome."

"The wind is blowing at 30 miles an hour right now," said Hunter as he took a reading with a wind gauge and reported his findings to the Hellroaring Fire headquarters via a hand-held two-way radio. "The fire is burning up Specimen Ridge, but we're still in an inversion, and the fire isn't moving very fast."

"Ten-four," came the response. "We're still in an inversion down here. Not much wind, but we are picking up a fair amount of ash and smoke."

Wind is a firefighter's nightmare. With 10-mile-per-hour winds, it's suicide to stand in front of a forest fire unless you want to attend your own barbecue.

On September 10, the Wolf Lake Fire (the northern front of the North Fork Fire) was five to eight miles from burning into the Hellroaring Fire. "If the fire jumps the Yellowstone River," said Hunter, "all our efforts over there will be for nothing."

That didn't happen. And at 6 P.M. on September 11, the Hellroaring Fire was declared 100 percent contained at 83,888 acres.

An Army Blackhawk helicopter at a landing zone to pick up soldiers who have been fighting fires all day. In the background, the fires can be seen on the distant ridge.

Facing page:
These soldiers in their helmets and fireproof trousers and shirts are checking their gear before loading up on buses at park headquarters, Mammoth Hot Springs.
Inset: *Barry Hottel, theForest Service "guru" who saved his troops during a firestorm.*

PATRICK CONE

U.S. Marine fire-fighters aboard a Chinook helicopter that will airlift them to a spike camp in the nearby mountains. Each man is carrying his sleeping bag, foam ground pad and personal equipment on a pack frame.

THE MARINES HAVE LANDED

Although there's always a lot of inter-service rivalry in the Armed Forces, Army troops from Fort Lewis, Washington were very happy when the Marines landed on September 13. Reinforcements are always a welcome sight in any war.

The first plane load of Marines from the 1st Battalion, 5th Marine Division (the "1/5") arrived at West Yellowstone Airport in a chartered jet. The second load, and subsequent loads, came in giant C-5A Galaxy transports that also brought along six or seven trucks and trailers loaded to the top with cold-weather gear.

It was pouring rain when 100 Marines from Camp Pendleton, California walked down the front ramp of the first transport and formed up.

"Company, Ahhh-*tennnn-hhuht!!*" shouted their commander. "Riightttt *face.* Column of files from the left...*Forrr-waaard, march.*"

For Major Jack Carter, the operations officer, this was a bittersweet homecoming. "I grew up in this area," said Carter as he strained to see a column of smoke on a ridgeline through the fog and rain. "My parents, grandparents and an aunt and uncle still live in West Yellowstone." Carter recalled spending a lot of time in Yellowstone National Park as a kid.

Unlike the Army, which had to fly in 1,000 extra pairs of boots and 2,000 pairs of socks and heavy-duty tents with heaters, Major Carter said the Marines came prepared for cold weather.

"A little snow or rain doesn't dampen the spirit of Marines," said Carter as he and his men boarded their trucks and headed for Madison Campground, where they pitched tents and unpacked gear.

The airport at West Yellowstone was a beehive of activity the day the Marines landed. The control tower was nothing more than a couple of wooden benches and a table atop the terminal area. A tent fly kept rain off tower operators who handled incoming traffic.

"This rain is a multi-million dollar asset to us right now," said Frank Mosbacher, the chief information officer for Yellowstone Fire Command, as he stood in the downpour and watched men and equipment emerge from the bellies of the big transports.

Mosbacher said the rain gave firefighters a chance to work right on the fire's edge and put in some good lines several hundred yards deep into the burned area, so that fire bosses could start looking at some containment work. The rain also enabled fire bosses to insert the Marines into action immediately.

The Marines who landed were eager to get to work. "Everybody's anxious to attack the fires," said Captain Dan McGinnis. "But first we've got to learn how to use equipment such as pulaskis, shovels and axes."

"Everybody can shovel dirt," said 1st Lt. Ian Ferguson, but he did not object to being taught how and when to shovel dirt. "We don't want any of our people getting hurt because they weren't familiar with the equipment."

The 1/5 received two days of classroom training in California from Los Angeles County firefighters who had seen fire duty in Yellowstone earlier in the summer.

"I volunteered for this," said Thomas Delaney of Munster, Indiana as he sharpened his K-Bar knife. "Relieves anxiety."

Clay Wild said he volunteered for fire duty to get away from the motor pool at Camp Pendleton, where he's a mechanic. Wild said more Marines wanted to come, but they had prior commitments.

In all, more than 1,300 Marines from the 1st Battalion, 5th Marine Division and 1st Battalion, 3rd Marine Division spent 30 days "mopping up" the North Fork Fire.

Between July 20 and September 30, 1988, the Department of Defense provided Army and Marine Corps personnel to assist civilian firefighters in the Greater Yellowstone Area, almost 12 million acres of land encompassing Yellowstone National Park and seven neighboring national forests. The peak military commitment on one day was 4,146 troops on September 17.

Fire managers praised the military participation in suppression activities, but stressed two areas to improve military assistance: increase mission understanding for the military so that they can be better prepared, and address the issue of pay discrepancy between troops and civilians.

SHADES OF VALLEY FORGE

A sign hanging on an Army tent in the Storm Creek Fire Camp outside Cooke City, Montana told a lot about life in the great outdoors. "Valley Forge West," proclaimed the homemade sign.

Rich Ballinger, a soldier from Fort Lewis, Washington put up the sign. Ballinger said, just like George Washington's men at Valley Forge during the Revolutionary War, his men needed boots.

"Well, it's not so much that our feet are cold," said Ballinger, "it's just the terrain we're climbing is destroying our boots." Ballinger, a clerk in HHB 1/11 Field Artillery, said the Army agreed to airlift 1,000 pairs of new boots and 2,000 pairs of socks into the camp.

When soldiers from Fourth Battalion of the 23rd Infantry at Fort Lewis first arrived at the Crandall Fire Base in Wyoming and were bussed to the Storm Creek Fire Camp outside Cooke City in late August, the days were warm and the nights were pleasant. But by the second week of September, the nights turned frosty, temperatures plummeted to the teens, and more men started lining up for sick call.

Base pay for an Army private is $671 per month, but some of the civilian firefighters made as much as $3,700 dollars per month. Even civilians who leased their pickup trucks to the Forest Service for $150 a day and 30 cents a mile made more than the GIs, and after a while that affected morale among the troops.

But Major-General Tom Cole, acting commander of the U.S. Sixth Army, didn't want to hear any complaints from his men. "Soldiers get paid to do their business," barked Cole, "besides, they're getting great food here, not that Army chow isn't good, but these interagency fire fellows are really catering great meals."

When Cole was informed the weather was taking a turn for the worse in Yellowstone, the Army commander ordered GP Medium tents with portable heaters flown in so his men would have warm places to sleep.

Until the cold-weather tents arrived, some soldiers at Madison Campground slept in cardboard boxes for warmth.

The Madison Fire Camp was one of the largest and best-equipped camps in Yellowstone. It was where the men and women who fought the North Fork Fire lived.

After a long, hard day of "humping up and down" rugged terrain and getting filthy, civilians and troops alike could shower in a portable trailer before dinner. But every meal was eaten outside under a big carnival tent.

ROSS SIMPSON

For firefighters, every day was the same. Out of the sack at 6 A.M., wolf down a quick breakfast and then saddle up for another back-breaking day of climbing hills and cutting brush.

After a hard day of digging fire lines, GIs dig into some of the delicious food prepared by civilian caterers at Madison Campground.

Sometimes the wind howled through the tent flaps, but the meals provided by caterers were piping hot and good. Pork chops, chicken and steak. Nothing but the best and all you could eat. Good food helped break the monotony of fire duty.

After breakfast, the troops boarded buses for a 45-minute ride to work in the nearby mountains. Every day was the same. Out of the sack at 6 A.M., wolf down a quick breakfast and then saddle up for another back-breaking day of climbing hills and cutting brush.

"Mopping up after them [civilian firefighters] is grunt work," complained Army 1st Lt. Kriston Herricks. "The Park Service should either let us fight fire or send us home." Although griping is half the fun of being a GI, the men and women from Fort Lewis dug in and did their job, and did it well. Fire commanders like Denny Bungarz, who supervised suppression efforts on the North Fork Fire, praised the military firefighters. "They're used to a little different organization than people you pull off the street," said Bungarz. "They're regimented, understand the chain of command, and are in very good physical condition." With a little training, Bungarz said, the soldiers from Fort Lewis were very effective in fighting the 1988 fires in Yellowstone National Park.

The air war

PATRICK CONE

"There's some smoke about 100 yards from where Freight-Train-Forty has dropped. Can we get a bucket in there?"

The radio call was from a helicopter coordinator aboard a Bell 206 leading an Army Chinook into a fire on Sepulchre Mountain just west of park headquarters at Mammoth Hot Springs.

"Two Chinooks have been dropping water non-stop today," said Bill Mundy, air operations director on the Mammoth Complex. "The coordinator locates the target and brings the Chinook in for the drop."

Seventy-seven helicopters dropped more than 10 million gallons of water on the Yellowstone fires. One bucket at a time. More than 7 million gallons of retardant were dropped by fixed-wing aircraft.

Two Wyoming Air National Guard C-130s equipped with Modular Airborne Fire Fighting Systems (MAFFS) made more than 204 air drops, dumping 5.4 million gallons of retardant on 14 separate fires. The Wyoming Air National Guard has two of only eight military MAFFS systems in the United States.

"Sometimes it's really spooky and tricky up there," said Curtiss Wainwright, as he walked to the operations office at the Mammoth helipad. "You get a lot of adrenalin rushes when the wind lets go of you, and you fall toward the trees."

Contract pilots like Wainwright are physically and mentally drained after six to eight hours of flying water in the wind. Small helicopters like the one Wainwright flies carry about 144 gallons of water in a collapsible canvas bucket attached to a 100-foot steel cable. Big helicopters like the twin-engine Army Chinooks can carry up to 1,000 gallons of water in their slings. "Picking up water from streams, ponds and lakes can be difficult," said Wainwright, "because it taxes a helicopter to the maximum."

A helicopter assigned to the Clover-Mist Fire crashed on September 20 while refilling a water bucket in a pond near the Crandall ranger station. One of the water bucket wires apparently got wrapped around one of the skids, causing the helicopter to flip upside down in the pond. The pilot, James Mitchell of CRT Helicopters in Apple Valley, California was sitting on the bank when a rescue team arrived.

"It gets a little squirrely," said Eric Boyce, another contract pilot on the Mammoth Complex, "when you're fighting the wind with a bucket of water and a full load of fuel on." Boyce said it was so smoky on some of the fires that it was

The greatest concentration of aircraft flying in support of fire suppression had to operate in limited air space with few navigational aids— just good old "seat of the pants" flying.

Top: *Just as their dads did during World War II, these Wyoming Air National Guardsmen painted their colors on the side of a C-130 that dropped retardant on the fires at Yellowstone.*
Center: *Bombs away!!!! A DC-6 drops chemical retardant on a stubborn fire that swept out of the Black Sand Basin and ran like a racehorse across a ridge south of Old Faithful on September 7, 1988. The retardant failed to halt the spread of this fire.*
Bottom: *Kris Woods, a civilian contract pilot who flew hundreds of missions dropping buckets of water from a sling attached to his Boeing Vertol, the civilian version of the military Chinook helicopter.*

Facing page: *A civilian Chinook helicopter airlifting a bucket of water to a fire as a smaller "chopper" slides underneath. These twin-engined helicopters could haul 1,000 gallons of water in each bucket.*

hard to keep out of the way of other helicopters.

Before the fires began to wind down, Congress passed historic legislation permitting the U.S. to contract with Canada for firefighters. About 400 Canadians from four provinces answered the call for help, bringing with them some of their aircraft.

Along with our neighbors to the north, the U.S. was able to field the greatest concentration of fixed-wing and rotor-wing aircraft in history flying in support of fire suppression—support which was flown in a relatively limited air space with little or no navigational aids, just lots of good old "seat of the pants" flying.

Many air crews, especially military crews, did not have experience flying fire missions, much less flying them in blinding smoke.

As Curtiss Wainwright climbed back into his chopper, he said, "This is the first day in the past month I can actually see where I'm going."

Miraculously, there were no mid-air collisions.

PATRICK CONE PHOTOS BOTH PAGES

Abandon ship!

MARK POLAKOF

It was the middle of night when the pilot came on the intercom with a brief announcement. "ALL CREW, PREPARE TO ABANDON SHIP."

But before Lt. Roy E. Thompson could repeat the message a second time, his co-pilot, Lt. James J. Highley, shrieked into the headphones, "GET OUT NOW! GET OUT NOW!"

Only one member of the crew was able to get out, and William F. McDonald, the bombardier, still can remember the night his buddies died. "I can still see them clawing the air trying to get out," said McDonald, who now lives in Buffalo, New York. "Those poor bastards must have died a hundred deaths in the few seconds before the plane hit the ground and exploded."

Second Lt. McDonald and his crew were assigned to the 2nd Bomber Command, 17th Wing, 2nd Air Force, 385th Bomb Group, 145th Squadron based at Lewistown, Montana. They had flown to Marysville, California where they completed their final, over-water training mission prior to shipping overseas, and were on their way back to home base in the wee hours of May 23, 1943 when their plane apparently iced up and crashed.

The pilot, co-pilot, navigator and flight engineer were the only ones awake as the Flying Fortress cruised along. McDonald and the rest of the crew had "sacked out" on the long night flight from California to Montana, lulled to sleep by four 1200-hp Cyclone engines.

There was no evidence of trouble until the pilot suddenly came on the intercom at about one o'clock in the morning and sounded the alarm, "Abandon ship."

"The next thing I remember," said McDonald, "I was way up in the air coming down in my parachute. I could see two big flames below where the plane crashed."

While working on the restoration of historic Old Faithful Inn, Andy Beck had heard rumors about a bomber crashing in Yellowstone National Park during World War II, but it wasn't until the young architect asked the "right questions of the right people" that he was able to obtain the coordinates of the crash site.

The North Fork Fire that threatened Old Faithful in 1988 laid bare the bones of the World War II-vintage B-17 bomber that had carried 10 young airmen to their deaths in 1943.

"We vaguely knew about all that stuff," said Yellowstone's maintenance chief, Tim Hudson, "but over the years, trees had grown up around it and it be-

The bomber that crashed in Yellowstone in '43 was similar to Sentimental Journey, a B-17 restored by the Confederate Air Force.

Facing page: *B-17 crash site uncovered by fires near West Yellowstone.*

came too hard to get to and too expensive to remove, so people forgot about it."

But the fires burned away the thick stands of lodgepole pine that had grown up around the wreckage, exposing tons of debris.

Much of the twisted aluminum and steel was loaded into helicopter slings and hauled four miles to a sorting area inside the park near West Yellowstone.

Dick Bahr, the air operations supervisor for Yellowstone National Park, supervised the removal of debris. "A helicopter pilot would hover over the wreckage," said Bahr, "while my four-man crew hooked up the cables." Bahr said the pilots did a lot of aerial reconnaissance at the crash site, and located the vertical and horizontal stabilizer on the tail section about a mile and a quarter from the main crash site.

Finding the tail section so far from the main crash site led Bahr to believe that the B-17 exploded in flight before it nosedived into the park, digging a 20-foot-deep crater in the ground.

Bill McDonald remembers seeing two large flames in the timber below his feet as he drifted down in his parachute. Although McDonald said the flames were a long way apart, he did not agree with Dick Bahr that the bomber exploded in mid-air.

"I won't say absolutely no explosion," said McDonald, "but I doubt there was, because I saw the plane hit the ground and explode."

A B-17 like the one that crashed in Yellowstone National Park had a gross weight of 46,726 pounds.

"The stuff we hauled out totaled about 25,000 pounds," said maintenance chief Hudson. "We flew all the bullets out first, then dumped and burned their powder." The biggest piece of wreckage recovered was a wing tip.

The Department of Defense gave Yellowstone permission to sell the wreckage as scrap to the highest bidder, but air operations supervisor Dick Bahr said only the aluminum was worth selling. The rest of the debris had no salvage value.

Park Historian Timothy Manns was one of the "right people" Andy Beck asked about the downed bomber. Using latitudes and longitudes provided by Manns, Beck and a friend, Jim Miller, who worked for a concessionaire in the park, hiked to the crash site in August 1982 by following old logging trails through a clearcut into drainages north of Jack Straw Basin.

"Only small parts were recognizable, such as gauges, radios, braces, brackets, oxygen tanks, access panels and machine guns," said Beck, who compiled a comprehensive report on the crash and donated it to the archives at Yellowstone.

The crash site is located about three and a half miles from where Beck and Miller parked their truck. Before the 1988 fire burned away 45 years of undergrowth, Beck said it was extremely difficult to crawl through dense stands of pine with runners that criss-crossed the ground. This kind of plant growth is sometimes called "dog hair" because of its unusual thickness.

Shortly after leaving Section 10, Township 14S, Range 5E, Beck and his buddy stumbled upon the first pieces of wreckage: several crushed practice bombs and an oxygen bottle. This was the initial orientation point for finding the other sites.

"We called Site Two, 'The Crater'," said Beck, "because it was a small circular area which appeared as if the aircraft simply dropped into the area and dug in rather than sliding through the trees."

Beck and Miller found seven .50-calibre machine guns at Site Two, each gun carefully demilitarized; however, there was plenty of live ammunition still scattered about the ground. Beck and Miller found three kinds of .50-calibre ammo: standard ball, tracer and armor piercing.

At Site Three, the major object was the outer third of the left wing, which was reasonably intact. Since most of the B-17—including the outer skin of the fuselage—was aluminum, the elements had done very little damage. Surprisingly, Beck found only minimal rust on the steel parts.

The major site, Number Four, contained the greatest variety of debris: engines, landing gear and personal equipment such as parts of leather jackets, canteens, soles of shoes and rings off parachute harnesses. Since there were no identifying markings on any of the personal gear recovered by Dick Bahr's men, it was sent to a mortuary and incinerated.

When I first learned that one member of the B-17 crew had survived the crash, I wondered if he was still alive. If so, where was he? And why hadn't anyone been able to find him?

A call to the Serviceman's Records Center in St. Louis was of no help in finding Lt. William F. McDonald, serial number 0734369. A fire in 1973 destroyed many of the records at the center.

A call to the Army desk at the Pentagon, however, put me in touch with the Veterans Administration in Washington. "If Lt. McDonald ever made a claim against the government," said a spokesman for the Army, "the VA probably has a record of it."

Sure enough, a computer sweep of VA records revealed that McDonald had made an inquiry in 1949.

At least I knew he had survived the war, but the VA could tell me only that the claim was from upstate New York. Pressing further, I learned the claim may have come from Buffalo, but was told that if McDonald was still alive, he had probably moved.

"Wrong," I told the VA. McDonald's generation went back to their hometowns after the war and rarely moved around the country. As it turned out, Bill McDonald moved one block in Buffalo after the war.

A call to Information in the Buffalo area turned up four separate listings for William F. McDonalds in the Buffalo telephone directory. The first three calls were non-productive, and I was just about ready to hang up on the fourth call when a voice answered the phone, "Bill McDonald."

Deciding to go for broke, I asked, "Did your B-17 bomber crash in Yellowstone National Park in 1943?" When McDonald replied, "Yes," I screamed, "I can't believe you're alive and I've found you!"

For the next hour or so, McDonald recalled the night his plane went down and how he was rescued by some park rangers. McDonald was equally surprised that the ranger who found him wandering around in the wilderness in 1943 also was alive.

It was impossible for Bill McDonald to recall every detail in the first interview, but over the next weeks, he reached back into the deepest, darkest recesses of his memory, and recalled with incredible clarity the story of his survival.

For Bill McDonald, the conversations were therapeutic. After each interview, he would return to his trunk of war memorabilia in the attic and search for information that might be helpful. It was during one search that he found the only photograph taken of his crew before they fell to their deaths.

"The plane was leaning to the left and shuddering as if stalling when the pilot and co-pilot screamed for us to get out," said McDonald as he recalled that fateful night in the spring of 1943.

"I was lying down over the forward escape hatch in the passageway that leads from the bombardier's station in the nose of the bomber to the flight deck where the pilot and co-pilot were sitting," said McDonald. Unlike other crewmen, who took off their parachutes during long night flights, he always wore his. Even when sleeping.

"We were supposed to wear our parachutes at all times," he explained, "but not everyone obeyed the rules." A couple of "close calls" while in training convinced McDonald never to take his parachute off.

During one of his first flights, the pilot decided to shake up his crew, and sounded a false alarm for them to abandon ship. McDonald had opened the forward hatch and was just about ready to bail out when the "All Clear" was sounded. McDonald came within a second of bailing out during a search mission when his plane spun out of control and came within a few hundred feet of plowing into the ground before the pilot recov-

Lacking his compass, ranger Ela marked the flaming crash's direction with matchsticks stuck into a railing.

Left: Bill McDonald, the lone survivor of the crash, at home in Buffalo, New York where he retired after a career as a high school English teacher.
Far left: Betty and Tom Ela, the former park ranger, heard the ill-fated B-17 pass over their cabin and crash in the park.

ered control. Ever since those two harrowing experiences, Bill McDonald never flew without strapping on a parachute. That and the fact he was sleeping over the escape hatch are the reasons he survived the crash about four miles south of West Yellowstone.

"The plane hit the ground within seconds after I bailed out," said McDonald, who believes the rest of the crew was trapped by gravity and couldn't get to their parachutes as the big bomber plunged nose first into the timber. Even though McDonald fell asleep over the forward escape hatch wearing his parachute, he may not have gotten out had he not been wearing his headphones and heard the pilot and co-pilot yell for everyone to get out.

Retired Yellowstone Park Ranger Tom Ela remembered the night the B-17 crashed. "My wife Betty and I had been to a birthday party when we heard the plane go over our cabin," said Ela, who now lives in Santa Fe, New Mexico. But the plane didn't sound right to Ela: "Its engines were laboring." He ran to Riverside Barns, an old stable for the early freight system in Yellowstone, to get a better view of the flames that lit up the sky on the horizon.

"When I got to the barn, I cussed myself because I had forgotten to bring my compass to get a bearing on the fire that was rapidly dying down in the distance," said Ela. But before the flames flickered out, the ingenious ranger reached into his pocket and pulled out a couple of Ohio Blue Tip matches and stuck them in a crack on the railing around the front of the barn, lining up both matchsticks with the flames. The next morning, before organizing a search party, Tom Ela returned to Riverside Barns and shot a compass reading on the crash using those two matchsticks.

Yellowstone National Park was heavily forested at that time so it was difficult for Ela to determine exactly how far away the plane crashed. But with a compass reading, Ela and other rangers were able to find the crash site without too much difficulty.

"There wasn't much left except a smoking hole and pieces of bodies lying around," said Ela, who found an airman's foot still in its flying boot. He also found a body still strapped in its parachute, so it appears at least one other crewman, like McDonald, wore his parachute, but because of the steep dive was unable to reach the Flying Fortress's escape hatch.

Normally a B-17 crew consisted of 10 men: pilot, co-pilot, navigator, bombardier, radio operator, flight engineer, two waist gunners, ball turret gunner and tail gunner, but there were 11 men aboard McDonald's aircraft the night it crashed.

"A couple of guys were returning to base with us," said McDonald, who remembers one of them, a young lieutenant who looked like actor George Brent. The other man was a sergeant. Both men were non-flying personnel: "Just a couple of hitchhikers," said McDonald.

There could have been 12 men on the ill-fated flight, but tail gunner Eddie Cavanaugh of Shamokin, Pennsylvania was sick and missed the training flight to California. However, Cavanaugh was assigned to another bomber crew after his was killed at Yellowstone, and saw combat in Europe. Bill McDonald remembers reading in *Stars and Stripes,* the GI newspaper, about a close call Cavanaugh had when his bomber was hit over Germany. But he never was able to find him after the war.

Before Tom Ela and several small groups of rangers set out to find the crash site, Assistant Chief Ranger Al Elliott called the nearest military base to tell them a large plane had crashed during the night.

"I suspected it was a military plane," said Tom Ela, who, like other rangers, was being trained as a civilian spotter during the war, "because of the way it sounded.

Rangers had reasonable doubt that there were any survivors, and the lone young airman had no food or blankets.

Dick Bahr's crew bagging up the World War II B-17 debris to be hauled out by helicopter.

Several engines. But we were never told what kind of plane was missing or how many men were aboard."

Although the Army Air Corps was close-mouthed about the crash, it did send a couple of single-engine observation planes to West Yellowstone to assist in the search for the bomber that had failed to arrive at Lewistown.

The search could have gone much smoother, but there was very little communication between the military and civilian authorities at Yellowstone after the crash. "We were all new at this kind of thing," confessed Ela, "but the Army wasn't saying much about the crash."

For example, if the Army had only inquired about a compass reading on the crash, the search planes would have been able to locate the wreckage on May 24, the day after.

Since there was some confusion about how many men might have been aboard the aircraft, Tom Ela organized a search for survivors. For two days, he climbed trees and hollered, HELLLLLL-OOOOOOO. On the second day—to his surprise—a call came back.

"I was really surprised that someone answered my call," said Ela, "because we had reasonable doubt there were any survivors." After all, the rangers had found 10 sets of dog tags on corpses at the crash site, the normal complement of a B-17 crew.

The man who answered Ela's call identified himself as Lt. William F.

McDonald, the bombardier. "Yeah, I remember this voice hollering in the wilderness," said McDonald, "and was I very glad to see someone."

McDonald was so stiff and sore by the time he was rescued, he could barely walk; his body ached after bailing out at low altitude. McDonald's fall was partially broken when his parachute snagged in a clump of trees, but he still hit the ground like a sack of potatoes.

"I landed in a snow bank, about two or three feet deep, and that cushioned the impact. But I had no idea where I was. It was pitch black in the woods, so I curled up on the ground and waited until daylight before moving."

Lt. McDonald heard a search plane late in the afternoon on May 24, the day after the crash. "It was a small Army plane, a Piper Cub flying low over the ridge." McDonald was able to attract the pilot's attention by taking off his shirt, tying it to a stick and waving the homemade flag. The plane dropped a note asking McDonald to signal if there were any other survivors.

Although McDonald was nowhere near the crash site, he shook his head, NO SURVIVORS. "I didn't see how any of my crew could have gotten out," said McDonald as he remembered the bomber was out of control when he opened the forward escape hatch and rolled out into the cold night air.

Before the military search plane left the area, the pilot dropped a burlap bag

Bill McDonald's crew. This photo was taken in 1943 at Lewistown, Montana.
Front row, *left to right: 2nd Lt. William F. McDonald, bombardier (Buffalo, New York), 2nd Lt. George A. Brast, navigator (Roosevelt, New York), 2nd Lt. Roy E. Thompson, pilot (Point Pleasant, New York), 2nd Lt. James J. Highley, co-pilot (Oklahoma City, Oklahoma).*
Back row, *left to right: S/sgt. Ed Cavanaugh, tail gunner (Shamokin, Pennsylvania), S/sgt. Donald Rice, radio operator (Henrietta, New York), S/sgt. Leo Thorn, gunner (Lake Charles, Louisiana), S/sgt. Lawrence Medlin, arm-gun (Brooklyn, New York), S/sgt. Alexander Jurkowski, Arm-Gun (Brooklyn, New York), S/sgt. Gilbert Underwood, Aer-Eng (West Orange, New Jersey).*

containing some canned goods. "But I didn't have a can opener," said McDonald, "so the food was useless. What I really needed was blankets to keep warm. I was half frozen, especially my feet."

Bill McDonald ate snow to keep from dehydrating and tried to stay on his feet during the night, walking to keep warm and occasionally slapping his sore shoulders with his bare hands.

"He was very, very cold, psychologically shot by the time he reached me and the search party," according to Ela, who still remembers the first question the bombardier asked him: "Where am I?"

When Ela told the young airman he was in Yellowstone National Park, McDonald couldn't believe it, but the bombardier was thankful to be alive. Ela said he could have wandered around the wilderness for days and never been found. "There aren't any streams to follow in the Madison Plateau where the plane crashed," said Ela. "It's a very bewildering area." Even if you do find a stream, it often leads to a sandy sinkhole.

After carrying Lt. McDonald about two miles to the crash site, where he identified the remains of his crew, Tom Ela and members of a just-arrived Army investigating team loaded the remains of the 10 dead men and some of the bomber's top-secret equipment (including the bombsight) onto horses and packed them out to the village of West Yellowstone. From there, the Army whisked McDonald to Pocatello, Idaho

where he was hospitalized with another member of his bombardier's class—who also had been rescued after bailing out over a wilderness area.

The Army team removed the crew's personal effects, and also "spiked" the .50-calibre machine guns by bending each of the barrels in the same direction and smashing the receivers on the left side with a sledgehammer, so no two parts could ever be re-assembled into a workable weapon. Team members also rolled the bomber's four engines into a deep ravine.

According to an Army Air Corps investigation, the pilot encountered rough air shortly after climbing to 15,000 feet over Reno, Nevada. The report states that the pilot, 2nd Lt. Roy E. Thompson, was flying on instruments at the time of the crash. Next to the line citing "Nature of Accident" is this notation: "Airplane encountered icing conditions." But there is another notation: "No definite knowledge of what happened."

Since the wreckage was scattered at four sites in Yellowstone National Park, Andy Beck also believes the B-17, tail number 42-30260, may have exploded in mid-air shortly after Lt. McDonald bailed out. But Beck says the real cause of the crash never may be known now that the wreckage has been hauled away from the crash site and the area returned to its natural state.

Andy Beck begged park officials to leave the crash site undisturbed and its

In 1963—during that same ill-fated month of May—a B-47 also crashed in Yellowstone National Park.

Architect Andy Beck standing behind the main landing gear of the B-47 jet bomber that crashed near Old Faithful in May 1963. This site was untouched by the Yellowstone fires.

location unpublished unless aviation aficionados requested specific information about the crash, because the crash site could not be seen from any road in the park and was accessible only by foot.

In a letter to Park Historian Timothy Manns in the summer of 1984, Beck wrote, "As a cultural resource, these sites probably will not be very valuable for years, so their best protection is to be left alone." However, Manns, who provided Beck with crash site coordinates, wished the Army Air Corps had "policed up the site" immediately after the crash in 1943. "It was, after all, an inappropriate intrusion," said Manns.

Beck disagrees. "What's garbage to us today is treasure to archaeologists at some date in the future."

Now that they've cleaned up the B-17 wreckage, park employees have set their sights on an even bigger reclamation project: a B-47 that crashed about 10 miles south of Old Faithful on May 3, 1963, killing three of the four-man crew.

Unlike the B-17, which exploded and burned on impact, the B-47 apparently came down in a flat spin like a leaf and did not break into a million pieces. There are very few pieces of the jet outside a 100-yard radius of the crash site.

The B-47 crashed after a mid-air collision with a tanker plane over Ashton, Idaho. The co-pilot ejected as soon as the aircraft passed through 10,000 feet. Why the other three crew members could not get out of the disabled bomber is still a mystery.

The bomber carried 10,000 gallons of jet fuel, but did not explode upon impact. Eight to 10 feet of snow in the area at the time of the crash may have cushioned the impact and reduced the danger of fire.

Like the bombardier on the B-17, the co-pilot on the B-47 was rescued, but only after spending a couple of nights alone in the wilderness. The B-47 wreckage is located in a small clump of trees along the Continental Divide, approximately 1.6 miles west of Douglas Knob and 1.9 miles south of Trischman Knob.

Tim Hudson, Yellowstone's maintenance chief, said he hoped to haul out about 85,000 pounds of junk. Andy Beck, who photographed the crash site in 1983, hoped Hudson would leave the wreckage intact.

Although bombardiers were in short supply in 1943, Lt. William McDonald never flew in combat after his close call in Yellowstone National Park. "The army apparently felt I had been through enough," said McDonald, who was assigned to the China-Burma-India theater of operations during World War II as a bombsight maintenance officer.

McDonald returned to Buffalo, New York after the war and fathered 15 children, seven sons and eight daughters, 14 of whom are still living. The Niagara University liberal arts major taught high school English, retiring from the public school system in 1980.

Bill McDonald had all but forgotten about his brush with death until his sister Theresa, a Roman Catholic nun in Erie,

Pennsylvania, sent him a newspaper clipping about a bomber being uncovered by the fires in Yellowstone. Although the article in the *Erie Times* on December 16, 1988 mentioned no survivor, McDonald's sister asked if that was his plane. McDonald said it was, but didn't make a big deal out of it. In fact, he asked his second wife, a writer, not to contact newspapers in Buffalo to let them know he was the lone survivor of that crash.

"I always felt guilty that I was the only one who survived," said McDonald, who had written to the family of each victim after the accident.

Why didn't he drop a line to the man who saved his life? "Truthfully," said McDonald, "I never thought about it."

But Bill McDonald said if I would give him Tom Ela's telephone number in Santa Fe, he would call the former park ranger and holler, "HELLLLOOOO."

It took McDonald more than two weeks to get up the courage to call the man who saved his life 46 years ago, but what a time he and Tom Ela had on the telephone.

"I want to thank you for saving my life," said McDonald, when Ela answered the telephone in Santa Fe.

"We exchanged addresses after reliving the experience," said Ela, "and perhaps some day we will meet again."

Before McDonald's B-17 was sold for salvage, ground up into small pieces and melted down, Dick Bahr, the operations supervisor at Yellowstone, sawed off the tip of one of the propellers and shipped it to me so I could have it engraved as a souvenir for Bill McDonald.

Like those on other bombers during the war, the propeller tip was painted yellow, and with the exception of some scratches, it looks as good as the night the prop dug itself into Yellowstone National Park. There's even some dirt still caked on the propeller which I couldn't bring myself to clean off before having the piece engraved with the aircraft's number and the date it crashed.

Every time Bill McDonald touches that propeller blade, he will remember how lucky he is to be alive.

During the 1988 Yellowstone fires, this B-17—the same type of plane that crashed in the park in 1943—was dropping fire retardant.

Praise for firefighters

PATRICK CONE

The following is the text of a letter Interior Secretary Donald Hodel sent October 13, 1988 to newspaper editors across the country praising the efforts of men and women who fought forest fires in the West that year.

To the Editor:

This summer long will be remembered for the forest fires that raged over much of the public lands in the West. Before the season is behind us, I want to extend my heartfelt thanks for the heroic efforts of the over 30,000 firefighters from across the country who, over the course of the past several months, risked their lives to try to control a natural disaster of unprecedented proportions. Whether called by a personal sense of duty or summoned by obligation, these men and women—working against insurmountable odds—showed exceptional courage and patriotism.

Many firefighters worked 12 to 14 hour shifts, with days consisting of hot, exhausting work battling fires, and nights spent in sleeping bags. In addition to facing the danger of intense blazes, falling limbs and oppressive smoke, they coped with everything from rockslides to angry yellowjackets. At the end of a workday, many firefighters carrying heavy gear hiked as much as ten miles before being picked up and returned to their camp.

Modern day forest managers and park rangers never have faced the conditions experienced this year in which millions of acres of aged timberlands were parched by four or five years of severe drought. Substantial portions of these great forests were living on borrowed time. Therefore despite all efforts, it was impossible to control the course of natural events.

We would be remiss if we did not learn from this experience. Now we begin the painstaking study to determine what, if anything, can be done to insure that we will not face devastating fires of this kind in the future. Work also must be done to help the rehabilitation of Yellowstone National Park and other affected areas.

Fortunately, much of Yellowstone escaped the raging fires—and, surprisingly, many acres of lush forestlands within burned areas were left unscathed. We are anticipating a great influx of tourists interested in seeing the extent of the damage and the progress of regrowth. Recreational opportunities will continue to abound.

Yellowstone will not be the same within our generation, but nature recovers from these events by rebirth of the old-growth forests and rejuvenation of forage and wildlife. It would be foolish to

In addition to facing the danger of intense blazes, falling limbs and oppressive smoke, they coped with everything from rockslides to angry yellow-jackets.

Top: *Civilian and military firefighters lighting backfires to deny approaching fire the dry fuel on the ground.*
Bottom left: *Despite the danger, there were few injuries among firefighters. Here a medic wraps the sprained ankle of one firefighter.*
Bottom right: *A sign outside Silver Gate, Montana says it all. Civilian and military firefighters were welcome guests in this gateway community.*

Facing page: *Exhausted military firefighter being airlifted back to base camp after a day on the fireline.*

say that the Yellowstone National Park forest fires were welcomed—but, over the course of the next decade, we may witness some beneficial effects.

This fact does not offer much solace for the local economies that have been disrupted, people displaced and painful losses suffered. And, those of us who love Yellowstone cannot help but view the events as a natural tragedy. But, the losses would have been much greater had it not been for the dedication and perseverance of the brave firefighters—and all who supported them in this difficult time. Again, to them. our thanks for doing an outstanding job.

/S/ Donald Hodel

YELLOWSTONE EPILOGUE

MICHAEL & BARBARA PFLAUM

STEVE DOWELL; BOZEMAN DAILY CHRONICLE

A sign at the edge of Yellowstone National Park said it all: EXTREME FIRE DANGER.

In 1988, the American West experienced the most severe fire season in recent history, during the driest summer on record. More than 68,000 wildfires burned that summer, compared with 49,000 in 1987.

Lightning started 49 fires in Yellowstone Park in 1988. Fourteen burned themselves out, 24 were contained or suppressed, and 11 natural starts burned together. Eight fires were burning inside the park when I arrived. Five of these eight burned into the park after starting on adjacent lands outside the park. Three of those five were lightning-caused, one was started by a human, and one was ignited when high winds blew a tree across a power line.

A team of nationally recognized fire behavior specialists, the "best in the business," was brought in to make daily predictions on the rate of spread of those fires, only to see those predictions substantially exceeded.

A recent analysis of fire scars on trees showed that large fires burned near Yellowstone Lake in 1750, the same year a young surveyor named George Washington was erecting a white post at an historic crossroads in the Shenandoah Valley of Virginia to lay out tracts of land for Lord Fairfax.

But not in recent history have so many large, uncontrolled wildfires burned across such remote, inaccessible sections of the West.

The 1988 fires at Yellowstone burned 988,925 acres, fewer than at first estimated, but the fires still created a massive smudge on the face of the nation's first national park. An estimated 1,000 miles of fire lines, five to seven major fire camps, 51 spike camps, tons of litter, 100 miles of roads, more than 600 miles of trails and 150 helispots required restoration. Some of them were restored and reseeded with winter wheat before the first snows fell that year.

But it will cost millions and take years to cosmetically restore Mother Nature's blackened face. A cooperative agreement has designated the National Park Foundation, a Washington-based nonprofit organization, to serve as the main repository for contributions.

For more information on how you can help, contact the Superintendent, Yellowstone National Park, Wyoming 82190.

When early trappers and frontiersmen like Osbourne Russell and Jim Bridger first came to the Yellowstone region in the early 1800s, the area was either burning or had recently burned. "That's why

70

they called the area around West Yellowstone, Burnt Hole," said local resident Bob Horte, who believes history has repeated itself.

Ecologists say Yellowstone National Park was simply "overdue" for another blowout, and once it started, man was not able to stop it. But just as it did in the days of Russell and Bridger, the forest will renew itself.

The Yellowstone fires were not only an "ecological event," but also a "media event" unequalled in the history of wildfires. Between July 21 and September 21, there were 3,000 media people in Yellowstone National Park. Every major newspaper in the United States, many foreign correspondents, major magazines and all the major radio and television networks in this country covered the historic fires.

As a network radio correspondent for the Mutual Broadcasting System, it was a time I shall never forget. From my first briefing upon entering the park at Grant Village, until the day I departed West Yellowstone to cover another disaster, Hurricane Gilbert in Mexico, I was told repeatedly that the fires were natural, "just Mother Nature's way of cleaning house."

As I drove around a curve in the road near Dunraven Pass and suddenly found myself in the midst of a firestorm sweeping over the highway, torching tall trees and partially blocking my way with falling snags, it was hard for me to think of fire as Mother Nature's way of preserving the diversity of plant and animal species. All I could think about was preserving one species, ME, and getting safely through that wall of fire before it exploded the car's fuel tank and roasted me alive.

It's funny how your mind works under severe stress. I wasn't so much concerned for my own safety as I was for the rental car I was driving. I suppose I take those contracts too seriously. As the incredible heat blistered the paint on the sides of the vehicle, I wondered who would pay for the car were it lost in the fire. Would I be liable? Fortunately, I was not injured and neither were any of my colleagues, some of whom also "stuck their necks out" to cover the "ecological event" of the past 300 years.

Looking west of Tower Junction, scene of some of the most intense fires, in September 1988. Mother Nature already has begun to cover up some of the damage she did that summer.

***Facing page, top:** Fires like this release the energy equivalent of 3 trillion BTUs per square mile.*
***Bottom:** A lone fire engine running a gauntlet of flame along the main road leading to Grant Village, as firefighters fought to save more than $70 million worth of structures. Only an outhouse was lost.*

The Montana Fire Story

by David Tippets

**USDA Forest Service,
Northern Region**

To understand 1988's phenomenal wildfires you have to look beyond the sensational headlines.

"Canyon Creek's Night of Terror... Explosion Onto Plains Overran All," said the Great Falls *Tribune,* describing the night that winds gusting to 60 miles per hour drove flames across 180,000 acres along the Rocky Mountain Front west of Great Falls.

For Montana and the Northern Region of the U.S. Forest Service, 1988 was the biggest fire year since 1910, even without Yellowstone National Park's blazes. But even more significant, 1988 witnessed the most prolonged "extreme" behavior since 1910.

Many factors combine to produce phenomenal fire years; but if one cause can be isolated to explain Canyon Creek's "Night of Terror," Yellowstone's "Black Saturday" and the other days when fires charred more than 100,000 acres, it was *wind.*

September 6, 1988 started like the previous mornings, said Craig Cowie, who was the strike-team leader for two 20-person crews of Montana Blackfeet Indians fighting the Canyon Creek Fire west of Great Falls. Crews crawled out of their sleeping bags and ate breakfast at the Elk Creek fire camp before daylight.

The fire-line supervisors huddled, sipping coffee from styrofoam cups at the morning briefing, while the crews hustled to fill canteens and pack lunches. That morning the people responsible for monitoring and predicting fire behavior warned the supervisors to prepare for increasing winds.

Just to be safe, the two crews in front cleared a safety zone for firefighters to escape into, but it was just a "matter of business," said Cowie, and he did not think they would actually need it.

By 3:00 P.M., the winds were gusting to between 40 and 50 miles per hour, and suddenly Cowie's crew had trouble keeping the fire from jumping across the fireline. By 4:00 P.M., they had intentionally burned all of the grass off the safety zone, to rob the fire of fuel before the intensity of the main fire front hit them. By 5:00 P.M., the world had come unglued: Fire spotted down the canyon and then burned back uphill toward the safety zone. The main fire front blew in from the other side.

By then, 107 firefighters had gathered in the safety zone—most of them close to the ground, where it was easier to breathe. The wind whipped burning embers and firebrands through the air. Divi-

sion supervisor Jerry Dombrovske ordered all the firefighters into their aluminum shelters for protection.

"They looked like rows of baked potatoes," Dombrovske said, describing men lying in their pup-tent–like bags. "We were untouched by the fire around us except for burning embers as big as coffee cups dropping around us."

Winds howled throughout the night, pushing the fire through the Elk Creek fire camp and across the prairie toward Augusta.

Haystacks, fences, sheds and a sawmill burned. The fire killed 265 cattle. No humans died or lost their homes, but loss of private property made this fire one of the biggest disasters of the '88 fire season.

Earlier in the summer, on August 20, the Storm Creek Fire on the Custer National Forest southwest of Billings, Montana had made an equally spectacular run on August 20.

"It ran up the Stillwater drainage about 10 miles in four hours…we had 70-mile-per-hour winds," said George Weldon, forester on the Beartooth Ranger District at Red Lodge, Montana.

Firefighters were trapped when the extreme winds hit, but they escaped serious injury by burning the grass off a large meadow to create a safety zone.

J. DOMBROVSKE, USFS

Earlier in the summer, on June 23, winds created a much more life-threatening situation: Eighteen members of the Wyoming Interagency Hotshot Crew were trapped while fighting the Brewer Fire in eastern Montana. With no time to burn out a safety zone, they crawled into their shelters and endured 15 minutes of terror while the fire burned through dense grass right up to and beneath their bags. Two men received minor burns; one suffered third degree burns; a fourth firefighter, Mark Sembach, was critically injured with respiratory burns and third-degree burns on hands, feet and legs.

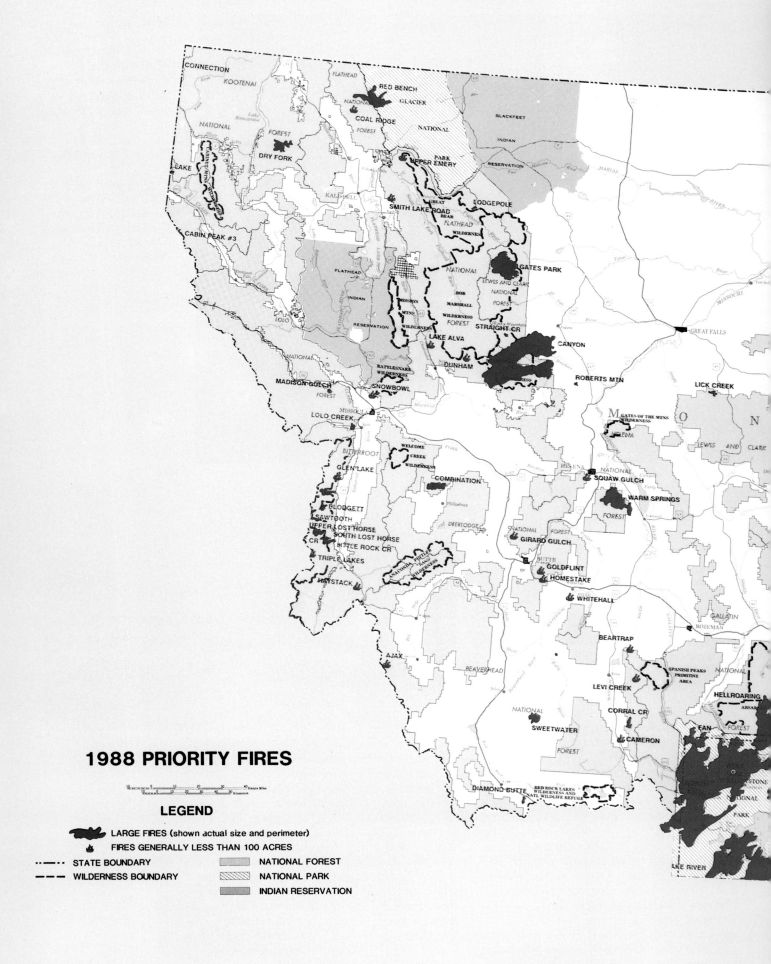

1988 PRIORITY FIRES

LEGEND

 LARGE FIRES (shown actual size and perimeter)

🔥 FIRES GENERALLY LESS THAN 100 ACRES

·—··—·· STATE BOUNDARY

– – – WILDERNESS BOUNDARY

NATIONAL FOREST

NATIONAL PARK

INDIAN RESERVATION

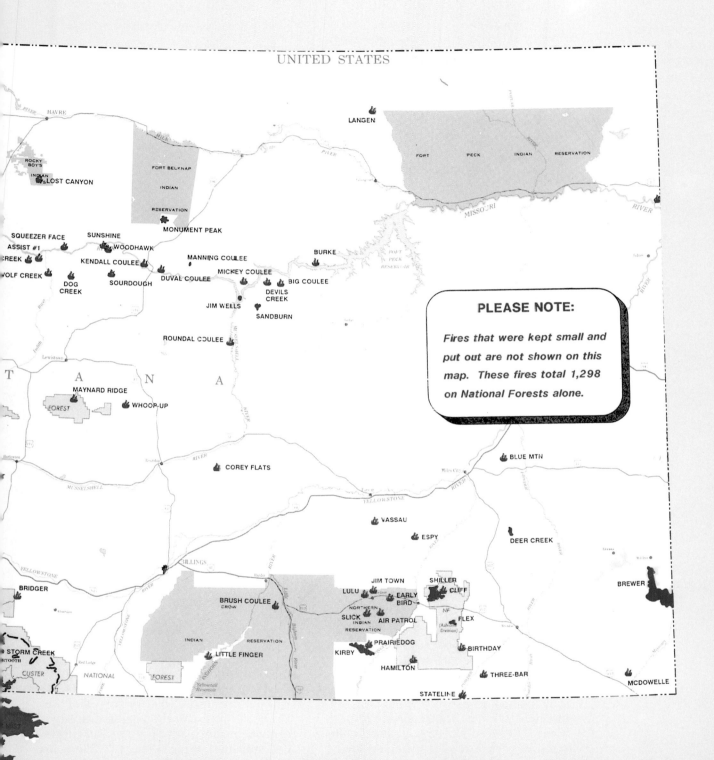

UNITED STATES

LANGEN

FORT PECK INDIAN RESERVATION

HAVRE

ROCKY BOY'S

INDIAN LOST CANYON

FORT BELKNAP

INDIAN

RESERVATION

MONUMENT PEAK

MISSOURI RIVER

SQUEEZER FACE

SUNSHINE

ASSIST #1

WOODHAWK

CREEK

KENDALL COULEE

MANNING COULEE

BURKE

WOLF CREEK

DOG CREEK

SOURDOUGH

DUVAL COULEE

MICKEY COULEE

BIG COULEE

DEVILS CREEK

JIM WELLS

SANDBURN

ROUNDAL COULEE

T A N A

MAYNARD RIDGE

FOREST

WHOOP-UP

PLEASE NOTE:

*Fires that were kept small and
put out are not shown on this
map. These fires total 1,298
on National Forests alone.*

BLUE MTN

COREY FLATS

VASSAU

ESPY

DEER CREEK

BRIDGER

JIM TOWN

SHILLER

CLIFF

BREWER

BRUSH COULEE

CROW

LULU

EARLY BIRD

SLICK

NORTHERN

INDIAN

RESERVATION

AIR PATROL

NF

(Ashland Division)

FLEX

STORM CREEK

CUSTER

NATIONAL

FOREST

LITTLE FINGER

KIRBY

PRAIRIEDOG

HAMILTON

BIRTHDAY

THREE-BAR

MCDOWELLE

STATELINE

MIST

75

MONTANA FIRES CHRONOLOGY

1988 Montana fires of more than 500 acres. This list includes the government agency on whose land the fire started, location, cause if available, and size. Acreage includes area over which fires spread; unburned areas often remain inside this perimeter acreage.

All figures provided by state and federal agencies. Adapted from the Great Falls (Montana) *Tribune*.

Deer Creek 1—BLM, near Miles City, controlled 6-23. 2,659 acres.

Brewer—BLM, 12 miles southeast of Ekalaka, lightning-caused 6-20-88, controlled 7-14. 57,500 acres in Montana, 800 acres in South Dakota.

Early Bird—Bureau of Indian Affairs (BIA), Northern Cheyenne Reservation, controlled 7-15. 22,000 acres.

Jim Town—BIA, Northern Cheyenne Reservation, controlled 7-15. 1,136 acres.

Flex—BLM, Custer NF, lightning-caused 7-12-88, controlled 7-16. 2,400 acres.

Schiller—BLM, Custer NF, lightning-caused 7-12-88, controlled 7-17. 15,250 acres.

Monument Peak—BLM, Little Rocky Mountains, 7-29. 5,774 acres.

McDowelle—BLM, west of Alzada, controlled 7-29. 3,500 acres.

Madison Gulch—FS, southeast of Alberton, controlled 8-1. 1,009 acres.

Rock Creek—FS, southwest of Hamilton, unextinguished campfire, controlled 8-5. 3,100 acres.

Brush Coulee—BIA, Crow Reservation, controlled 8-12. 1,500 acres.

Lodgepole Creek—FS, Great Bear Wilderness south of Glacier Park, lightning-caused on 8-5-88, controlled 8-13. 640 acres.

Sweetwater—State, 14 miles southeast of Dillon, controlled 8-14. 8,000 acres.

Little Finger—BIA, Crow Reservation, lightning-caused 8-11-88, controlled 8-14. 1,755 acres.

Diamond Butte—State, 20 miles southwest of Dillon, controlled 8-19. 1,000 acres.

Lulu—BIA, Northern Cheyenne Reservation, controlled 8-19. 780 acres.

Vassau—State, 12 miles southeast of Forsyth, lightning-caused, controlled 8-19. 800 acres.

Air Patrol—BIA, Northern Cheyenne Reservation, controlled 8-20. 4,050 acres.

Slick—BIA, Northern Cheyenne Reservation, controlled 8-21. 8,825 acres.

Espy—State, east of Colstrip, lightning-caused, controlled 8-22. 5,460 acres.

Lost Canyon—BIA, Rocky Boy Reservation, lightning-caused 8-16-88, controlled 8-22. 4,500 acres.

Corey Flats—State, Bull Mountains east of Roundup, controlled 8-22. 3,029 acres.

Kirby—State, south of Northern Cheyenne Reservation, started 8-19-88, controlled 8-26. 12,795 acres.

Iron Claim—FS, Little Belt Mountains 12 miles southwest of Stanford, started 8-24-88, controlled 8-27. 1,475 acres.

Cameron—State, south of Ennis in Madison Range, controlled 8-27. 1,100 acres.

Two Dot—State, six miles south of Martinsdale, controlled 9-1. 5,240 acres.

Warm Springs Creek—FS, Elkhorn Mountains southeast of Helena, caused by vehicle fire 8-9-88, controlled 9-3. 46,900 acres.

Lolo Creek—FS, 15 miles southwest of Missoula near Lolo, man-caused on 8-25-88, controlled 9-5. 2,230 acres.

Corral Creek—FS, on Beaverhead Forest west of Yellowstone Park, controlled 9-6. 2,860 acres.

Combination—FS, between Philipsburg and Drummond, controlled 9-7. 11,262 acres.

Lick Creek—FS, Logging Creek area west of Monarch, vehicle fire 9-2-88, controlled 9-8. 1,090 acres.

Dry Fork—State, lightning-caused 8-25, 20 miles east of Libby, controlled 9-16. 12,917 acres.

Red Bench—FS/Glacier Park, started 9-6-88 near Polebridge, cause under investigation, contained by weather 9-20. 35,400 acres.

Canyon Creek—FS, lightning-caused in Scapegoat Wilderness 6-25-88, weather contained by 9-20. 247,000 acres.

Gates Park—FS, 35 miles west of Choteau, lightning-caused 7-11-88, weather contained by 9-20. 50,850 acres.

Hellroaring—FS, northeast of Gardiner in Absaroka-Beartooth Wilderness, man-caused, contained at 81,950 acres.

Storm Creek—FS, northwest of Gardiner, Absaroka-Beartooth Wilderness, lightning-caused, contained 9-17. 107,847 acres.

Winds frustrated crews on the Warm Springs Creek Fire that broke out on August 9 in the Elkhorn Mountains within sight of Helena—Montana's capital. It was nearly three weeks before fire officials could claim success in stopping the fire's advance. By then, 37,600 acres had been burned. Residents of several small communities were forced to evacuate; two homes and 11 cabins were destroyed. Six C-130 slurry bombers and 2,900 firefighters attacked the inferno that had begun when a vehicle engine fire ignited roadside vegetation at the head of Warm Springs Creek. Then, with barely a pause to shower and change, firefighters headed for the 10,000-acre Maxville area fire in the Flint Creek Range north of Philipsburg. Planes that had flown retardant runs on the Warm Springs Creek Fire continued to use the Helena Airport as they attacked the Maxville fire.

Winds gusting to 50 miles per hour on the Red Bench Fire in Glacier National Park and the Flathead National Forest whirled fire across the North Fork of the Flathead River. But the biggest tragedy came days later, after the fire and winds had subsided, when a snag fell, killing firefighter Patrick David.

A similar accident on October 11 took the life of Edward Hutton. He was on mop-up duty at the Clover-Mist Fire when a snag fell on him. Earlier, on August 10, while battling the Brush Coulee Fire near Crow Agency in eastern Montana, seasonal firefighter Cheryl Old Horn Deputee died when the pumper truck on which she was standing rolled.

Without minimizing the tragedy and

near-tragedy of the '88 season, organization, communication, cooperation, transportation and improved technology saved lives in ways unheard of in 1910.

By September, 17,000 people fought the blazes in the Northern Region and in the Greater Yellowstone Area. An additional 2,000 people worked feeding, supplying and transporting firefighters. At one point, 6,000 soldiers joined in the struggle. The Canadian Air Force crossed the border with aircraft, equipment and crews.

Yet it was Mother Nature who finally put out the fires: September snow storms brought the infernos of 1988 to an end.

JUMPERS' LONG SEASON

During rainy years smokejumpers go crazy with boredom, said Mike Plattes, Smokejumper Operations Manager at the USDA Forest Service's aerial fire depot in Missoula, Montana. But in 1988, boredom was not a problem.

Plattes stated that 1988 was the year the fire season started in February; the year jumpers often worked 30 to 40 hours straight; the year the fires burned all night, into the next day, into the next week and kept going until the snows of September.

For the first time in 16 years as a jumper, Plattes assigned mandatory days off to the elite firefighters that he supervises. Other years, said Plattes, the weather always had given jumpers a reprieve after two or three weeks—but not during the summer of 1988.

Jumpers rarely complain. Being tough is part of the aura; so Plattes had to watch his men's faces as they returned to base. Those who looked too tired to work safely received a day off—just long enough to sleep, wash socks and underwear, repack gear and be ready to jump again.

Terry Williamson, a seasoned jumper from Missoula, said that, to him, extreme fire behavior was the most memorable thing about '88. Fires were still running in the crowns at 2:00 A.M., said Williamson. By 4:00 A.M., spot fires would erupt way out in front of the main fire, he added.

Smokejumpers dig fireline faster than any other kind of fire crew—and dig it so that it holds. But 1988 presented new challenges, said Williamson. Vegetation was so dry and burned so intensely that fires slopped over their lines regularly. There just were not enough firefighters to hold all the lines, said Williamson, and on many days, they had to start building new line all over again.

During a typical year, a lightning strike may require two jumpers, who

work furiously for a couple of hours, chopping out brush and scraping away fuel until they contain the fire. The night is spent mopping up. The hardest job is usually the long hike out, carrying more than 100 pounds of gear on their backs.

But in 1988, the scenario changed. Williamson recalled a few times when, by the time the plane with two jumpers arrived, the fire already had exploded to 70 to 100 acres, sending a column of smoke 10,000 feet into the sky.

In 1988 more jumpers than usual were needed on every new start, and they dug line not just for hours, but for days.

No, jumpers were not bored in 1988.

Smokejumpers faced unprecedented challenges because of drought conditions in 1988.

BERT LINDLER

KAREN WESTLY

Above: *Charred forest and grasslands off Haystack Butte, looking toward the Rocky Mountains.*
Above right: *Aerial re-seeding is part of the rehab program after fire on the national forests.*
Right: *This photo was taken less than three hours after the Warm Springs Creek Fire began, and shows the area where it started.*
Below: *Mop-up at the Warm Springs Creek Fire.*

WILLIAM R. SALLAZ

RICK GRAETZ

COURTESY USDA FOREST SERVICE

JOHN BALL

WILLIAM R. SALLAZ

SCOTT CRANDELL

Top left: *The Red Bench Fire came close to destroying this local gathering spot treasured by North Fork residents.*
Top right: *From the grounds of the Nature Conservancy Ranch on Elk Creek south of Augusta, looking toward the Canyon Creek Fire.*
Above: *Retardant drop, Warm Springs Creek Fire.*
Left: *Rehabilitation work begins following the Red Bench Fire.*
Overleaf: *Arrowleaf balsamroot and old snags show natural healing in progress.*